Popular Mechanics

JOINTER & PLANER FUNDAMENTALS

Rick Peters

Hearst Books
A Division of Sterling Publishing Co., Inc.
New York

Production Staff

Design: Triad Design Group

Cover Design: Celia Fuller

Photography: Christopher J. Vendetta

Cover photo: Powermatic

Illustrations: Bob Crimi

Copy Editor: Barbara McIntosh Webb

Page Layout: Sandy Freeman

Index: Nan Badgett

The written instructions, photographs and illustrations, and projects in this volume are intended for the personal use of the reader and may be reproduced for that purpose only. Any other use, especially commercial use, is forbidden under law without the written permission of the copyright holder.

Every effort has been made to ensure that all information in this book is accurate. However, due to differing conditions, tools, and individual skills, the publisher cannot be responsible for injuries, losses, or other damages which may result from the use of the information in this book.

Note: The safety guards were removed for clarity in many of the photographs in this book. Make sure to always use all safety devices according to the manufacturers' instructions.

Library of Congress Cataloging-in-Publication Data
Peters, Rick.
  Popular mechanics jointer & planer fundamentals: the complete guide / Rick Peters
        p. cm
  Includes index
  ISBN-13: 978–1–58816–556–5
  ISBN-10: 1–58816–556–6
1. Woodwork—Equipment and supplies. 2. Jointer (Woodworking machine) 3. Planer saws. 4. Planing-machines. I. Title. II. Title: Jointer & planer fundamentals. III. Title: Popular mechanics jointer and planer fundamentals.
  TT186.P46123. 2007
  684'.08—dc22
                                                    2006032762

10 9 8 7 6 5 4 3 2 1

Published by Hearst Books
A Division of Sterling Publishing Co., Inc.
387 Park Avenue South, New York, NY 10016

Popular Mechanics and Hearst Books are trademarks of Hearst Communications, Inc.

www.popularmechanics.com

For information about custom editions, special sales, premium and corporate purchases, please contact Sterling Speical Sales Department at 800-805-5489 or specialsales@sterlingpub.com.

Distributed in Canada by Sterling Publishing
c/o Canadian Manda Group, 165 Dufferin Street
Toronto, Ontario, Canada M6K 3H6

Distributed in Australia by Capricorn Link (Australia) Pty. Ltd.,
P.O. Box 704, Windsor, NSW 2756 Australia

Manufactured in China

Sterling ISBN 13: 978–1–58816–556–5
ISBN 10: 1–58816–556–6

Contents

ACKNOWLEDGMENTS

For all their help, advice, and support, I offer thanks to:

Christian Chenier and Norm Frampton, at General International, for supplying a General jointer and planer/molder and for technical assistance.

Bob Varzino, at WMH Tool Group (Jet and Powermatic), for supplying a Jet jointer and planer/molder and for technical assistance.

Brian Remsberg, for Ryobi Tools USA, for supplying a Ryobi portable planer and technical assistance.

Brett Willi, for Delta Machinery, for supplying a Delta bench-top jointer.

Jason Feldner, with Bosch Tools, for supplying a cordless portable power planer.

Lisa Clark, at Sunhill Machinery, for providing a spiral cutterhead.

Michele Spiegel, at Amana Tool, for providing replacement jointer and planer knives.

Christopher Vendetta, for taking great photographs under less-than-desirable conditions and under tight deadlines.

Bob Crimi, for superb illustrations.

Sandy Freeman, whose design and page layout talents are evident on every page of this book.

Barb Webb, copyediting whiz, for ferreting out mistakes and gently suggesting corrections.

Heartfelt thanks to my constant inspiration: Cheryl, Lynne, Will, and Beth.

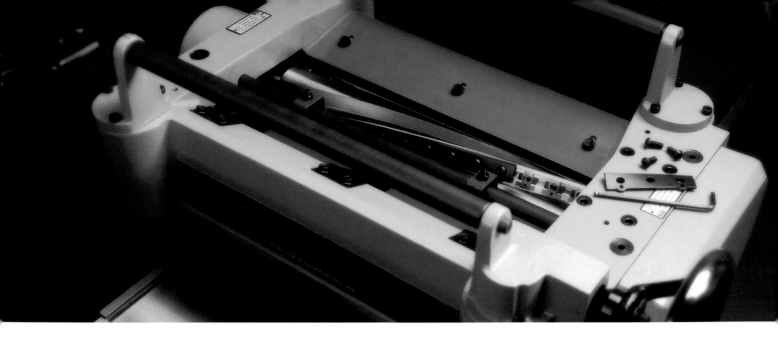

INTRODUCTION

When novice woodworkers start building projects for the first time, they often wonder why many of their projects don't turn out like they had hoped. Quite often there are gaps in glue joints and between parts that were joined together. They often don't blame the wood, because it was purchased from a reputable dealer and came surfaced on all four sides. They assume that the lumber is square and flat. So a common solution for non-fitting parts is for them to use bigger clamps, thinking they can force the wood into submission. Not so.

The problem was that it actually *was* the wood. There wasn't anything wrong with it—it wasn't defective. It was just wood, and wood moves. It constantly reacts to changes in humidity and will continue to move and swell after it has been dried and surfaced. The thing is, no matter where you buy your wood, and regardless of its quality, it's never going to be perfectly flat and square. Never. The only way it gets there is if you make it so. And the two tools that you'll need for this are the jointer and the planer.

A jointer produces a true, flat face that is the foundation of square stock. With the same machine, you then create perfectly perpendicular edges. The planer comes next, to create absolutely parallel faces. The end result: square stock that when used for your projects will make everything you build go together easier and stay together longer.

In this book, we'll help identify which jointer and planer is best for you (as well as accessories). We'll cover basic and advanced techniques, and show you how to make jigs and fixtures to expand the capabilities of both tools. Maintenance and repair is covered in detail so that you can keep these foundation tools in tip-top shape. And the final chapter details projects that you can build using a jointer and planer. Armed with this information, we hope that you'll use these tools with greater confidence to handle a wide variety of jobs around the home and shop.

—James Meigs

Editor-in-Chief, **Popular Mechanics**

1 Choosing a Jointer or Planer

No matter where you buy your wood, it won't be square. Period. The only way it gets square is if you make it so. And the two tools that you'll use to do this are the jointer and the planer. These two tools, along with the table saw, make up the triangle of tools that form the foundation of any woodworking shop. It won't matter how sharp your tools are or how precise your jigs are—if the stock isn't square to begin with, the project likely won't turn out right. In this chapter, we'll describe how jointers and planers work so you can better judge the different types and models out there. We'll identify the main types of jointers and planers: bench-top, stationary, and industrial. Then we'll wade through the many features to consider when looking to purchase a jointer or planer.

Jointers and planers create flat, square stock that is the foundation of every successful woodworking project. Both are available in a wide variety of sizes and varying capabilities.

Jointer Basics

A jointer consists of two parallel tables with a spinning cutterhead in the middle that shaves off small amounts of wood from a workpiece that's passed over it, as shown in the drawing below.

Stock is fed into the cutterhead via the infeed table, and the outfeed table supports the freshly jointed workpiece during and after the cut. The knives of the cutterhead (anywhere from two to four) and the outfeed table are set to the same height. The infeed table on all jointers slides up and down to control the depth of cut when the height-adjustment handwheel or knob is rotated. The outfeed table may or may not be adjustable. An adjustable outfeed table tends to make it easier to install and align the knives in the cutterhead.

The cutterhead is rotated by a belt connected to the motor via a set of pulleys. Most jointers employ a totally enclosed fan-cooled induction motor; smaller bench-top jointers often use an induction motor (for more on motor types, sizes, and horsepower ratings, see pages 13–14).

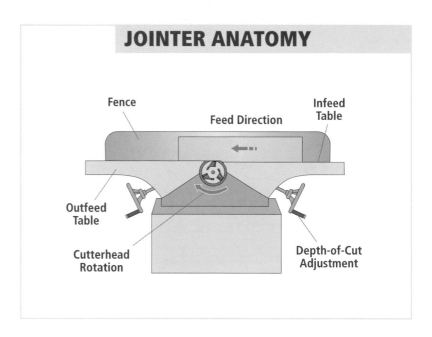

JOINTER ANATOMY

Fence

Feed Direction

Infeed Table

Outfeed Table

Cutterhead Rotation

Depth-of-Cut Adjustment

Bench-Top Jointers

Bench-top jointers like the one shown here have limited use in the woodworking shop, primarily because of their short bed and underpowered motor. They do, however, work fine for short stock on limited runs—we know a number of woodcrafters who find this type of jointer more than adequate for their needs—this is especially true for those folks for whom space in the shop is at a premium. The diminutive size of a bench-top jointer makes it easier to shoehorn it into a small space.

But for woodworkers who are building furniture, the short bed length is a real problem: It's difficult to accurately joint long boards—even with some form of additional support (see page 47). Although these small jointers often have a reasonably wide bed (6"), you'll be hard-pressed to get a smooth cut when face-jointing stock that wide. In the first place, the universal motor just doesn't have the power to handle the job. If you do try to make this cut, the already loud motor will screech trying to handle the load. The only advantage to a universal motor is that it's easy to vary the speed—most small jointers have a speed adjustment that will allow you to better match the planing speed to the material.

BENCH-TOP JOINTER ANATOMY

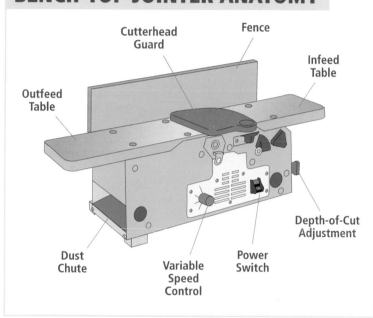

Cutterhead Guard

Fence

Infeed Table

Outfeed Table

Depth-of-Cut Adjustment

Dust Chute

Variable Speed Control

Power Switch

PORTABLE POWER PLANERS

Portable power planers are technically neither planer nor jointer. Although the name implies that a power planer is a planer, it isn't. It's not capable of thicknessing stock so that the opposite faces end up parallel. A power planer acts more like a jointer, except that you move the tool over the workpiece instead of the other way around. Since the "bed" of a power planer is so short, it can't straighten or flatten boards like a jointer. A power planer really is a motorized hand plane. It's a terrific tool for removing a precise shaving from a project. Trim carpenters love these because they can remove a lot of material in a short time.

Stationary Jointers

A better choice for the average woodworker is a stationary or floor-model jointer, as the length of the bed is better matched to the width of the table. The table width on most stationary jointers ranges from 6" to 8". Many woodworkers find that a 6" jointer will do the job; but if funds and space permit, an 8" jointer is a better choice.

As the bed widens, the tables lengthen. And the longer the tables, the more accurate and easy it is to straighten and flatten lumber. Smaller 6" jointers are typically driven by a $^3/_4$- to 1-hp induction motor, while the larger 8" models typically have a $1^1/_2$- to 2-hp motor. Stationary jointers are available with open or closed stands. We prefer closed stands, as we find it easier to control dust and chips. Most models come with a dust port so that you can hook it up to a dust collector or shop vacuum. In addition to having wider, longer tables and beefier motors, most 8" jointers have a larger-diameter cutterhead that holds more knives. The larger the cutterhead, the more it cuts nearly parallel to the grain—and the smoother the cut. More knives at a higher rpm also mean a smoother cut.

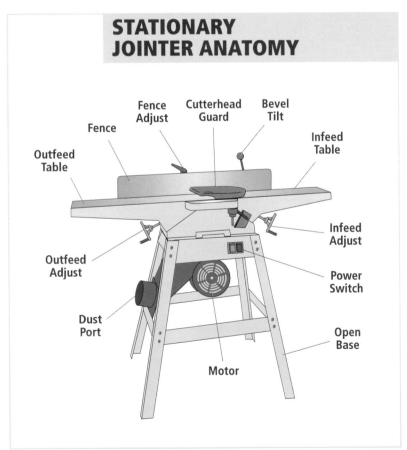

STATIONARY JOINTER ANATOMY

Fence Adjust · Cutterhead Guard · Bevel Tilt · Fence · Infeed Table · Outfeed Table · Infeed Adjust · Outfeed Adjust · Power Switch · Dust Port · Open Base · Motor

Industrial Jointers

Most woodworkers can't justify the expense or shop space needed for an industrial jointer. Additionally, most industrial-quality jointers use large motors (3 to 5 hp) that require at minimum 220-volt power; some require 440-volt, and many are three-phase. Not something the average woodworker has in the shop. And you'll need a forklift to unload one of these beasts, as they typically weigh anywhere from $3/4$ ton up to a full ton.

That said, they really are a joy to use. Table widths vary from 12" to 16", and bed lengths vary anywhere from 84" to 102"—that's $8^{1}/_2$ feet long! And because they're so long and heavy, vibration is virtually nonexistent, so you can smoothly joint long, wide, or heavy lumber with ease.

TYPICAL JOINTER CAPACITIES

Trying to decide which jointer is best for you? Here's a quick comparison of capacities of the varying jointer types: bench-top, stationary, and industrial. For more detailed specifications, see pages 18–19.

Jointer Type	Maximum Depth of Cut	Maximum Width of Cut	Bed Length	Motor Size
Bench-top	$1/_8$"	4" – 6"	24" – 30"	$1/_2$ – 1 hp
Stationary	$1/_2$"	6" – 8"	46" – 70"	$3/_4$ – 2 hp
Industrial	$3/_4$"	12" – 16"	84" – 102"	3 – 5 hp

Jointer Features

There are plenty of features to look for when shopping for a new or used jointer. These include table width and length, depth of cut, motor type and size, cutterhead guard, infeed/outfeed table adjustments, rabbetting ledge, fence tilt, and dust collection.

Table width and length

The width of a jointer's table determines the maximum cut, as illustrated in the drawing below right. Many woodworkers opt for a 6" jointer because of cost but end up wishing they'd purchased an 8" jointer. The extra 2" makes a big difference when preparing rough stock—you'll often encounter boards that are wider than 6". With a 6" jointer, you'll need to rip the board before you can surface it. And the longer the tables, the easier it is to flatten and straighten lumber. With short tables it's easy to end up with a bowed board, as the ends of the board aren't in constant contact with the tables. If space is problem, you can try supporting the workpiece with outfeed rollers, but they won't do as good a job as long tables.

Depth of cut

The maximum depth of cut on a jointer is established by the amount of travel in the infeed table, as illustrated in the bottom drawing. For most jointing operations, how deep a cut you can take is irrelevant, as it's best to take a series of light cuts—it's easier on the jointer and will produce a smoother finish with less chance of tear-out or chip-out. Only in a production environment does maximum depth of cut ever come into play. The standard $1/8$" max cut on most jointers will rarely limit what the average woodworker can accomplish.

Motor type and size

The two types of motors you'll find on jointers are universal and induction.

UNIVERSAL MOTORS. Bench-top jointers utilize universal motors and can tackle only small jobs (middle photo on page 13). Universal motors are compact, have a high starting torque, and run at high rpm. The downside to a universal motor is that it doesn't have anywhere near the continuous load capabilities of an induction motor. This means they stall easily when making an aggressive cut, cutting into thick stock or dense woods. In most cases, you can still make the cut, as long as you decrease the rate at

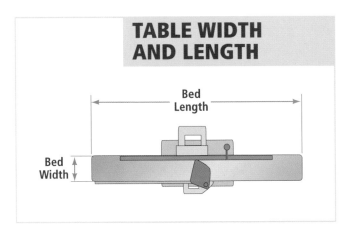

TABLE WIDTH AND LENGTH

Bed Length

Bed Width

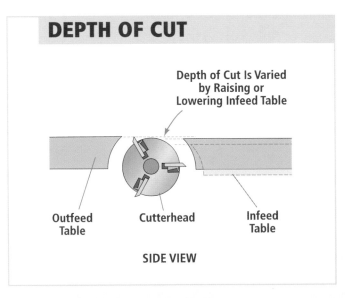

DEPTH OF CUT

Depth of Cut Is Varied by Raising or Lowering Infeed Table

Outfeed Table

Cutterhead

Infeed Table

SIDE VIEW

which the wood is fed into the blade. Often this slower feed rate is so slow that it'll cause burning. And when a universal motor is continuously bogged down like this, there's a very real danger of burning out the motor.

INDUCTION MOTORS. Stationary jointers feature a large induction motor designed for heavier loads. They spin the cutterhead via a belt (bottom photo). Induction motors are heavy and bulky, but powerful. Best of all they're virtually maintenance-free. Most have winding taps that allow you to wire the motor for 110- or 220-volt operation. Most 6" jointers use a 1-hp induction motor—big enough for most jobs. On the other hand, if you tend to work with thick stock and/or work a jointer hard, you're better off with a larger motor. A typical 8" jointer uses a 2-hp induction motor that is powerful enough to joint the full bed width in a single pass.

The higher the horsepower and current rating, the stronger the motor. Note that most 8" and larger jointers require 220 volts to run. This is another reason that many woodworkers end up with a smaller 6" jointer—these run off 110 volts.

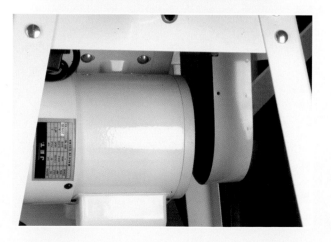

HORSEPOWER 101

Horsepower is the amount of work done over time. Generally, when used to describe a tool, horsepower is an indication of how capable the tool is of performing its tasks. The rated horsepower of a tool is usually the torque level at which the motor can be run *continuously* without exceeding the temperature at which the winding insulation beaks down.

No motor produces usable horsepower unless it is slowed down by applying a mechanical load. With a universal motor, the manufacturer often labels horsepower as "developed" horsepower. This is an attempt to mislead the consumer into thinking their products are more capable than they really are. Developed horsepower may be 2 to 5 times the continuous-duty rating of a motor. The term "develops 3 hp" is just meaningless marketing hype—use the amperage rating instead. As a rule of thumb, the higher the amperage, the more powerful the motor. (Amperage ratings can be found on the motor label.)

Guards

One of the most often overlooked features of a jointer is its guard. Look for one that has a strong return mechanism to guarantee that the knives are never exposed when jointing. Also, make sure that the guard is removable. There are some techniques where it will get in the way—rabbeting (see pages 82–83), raising panels (see pages 88–89), and face-jointing wide stock. The guard should also be adjustable in height and must cover the knives regardless of the position of the fence—move the fence to both extremes to ensure that it does. We prefer a guard with an easy-to-use finger pull on top (like the one shown in the top photo) for swinging the guard out as needed, versus the dished hand-hold of the guard shown in the middle photo.

Adjustable outfeed table

On some larger jointers, you'll often find that the outfeed table is adjustable, as shown in the bottom photo. The big advantage to this is that the cutterhead knives can be sharpened in place, and the outfeed table can then be lowered to match their new height.

Infeed table adjustment

The infeed table has grooves underneath its body that fit over the gibs in the base of the jointer, as illustrated in the middle drawing. A threaded rod, which terminates in the infeed table handwheel adjustment, interlocks with a threaded portion of the base to control movement.

Since the infeed adjustment is the main adjustment for a jointer, it's important that the adjustment mechanism be both easy to use and accessible. Our preference is for a handwheel (like the one shown in the top left photo), but some woodworkers prefer the lever style common on some models (top right photo). Regardless of the handle or lever, make sure that there's a positive locking mechanism that will prevent the table from shifting out of position while it's in use.

Rabbeting ledge

Another feature to look for in a jointer is a rabbeting ledge, like the one shown in the bottom photo. A rabbeting ledge is a notch milled into the side of the outfeed table that allows the unrabbeted portion of the workpiece to clear the table. Rabbeting on the jointer is a terrific way to produce clean, crisp rabbets—as long as the rabbet runs with the grain.

For more on rabbeting, see pages 82–83.

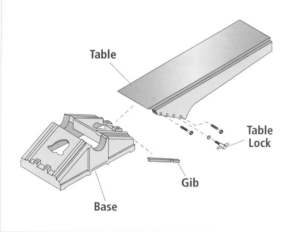

INFEED TABLE ANATOMY

Table

Base

Gib

Table Lock

Fences and fence adjustment

A flat table is one-half of the critical equation that creates perpendicular adjacent edges. The fence is the other half. The fence on a quality jointer should be large, heavy, and well machined. It should be easy to adjust back and forth across the tables, as well as having a positive locking mechanism.

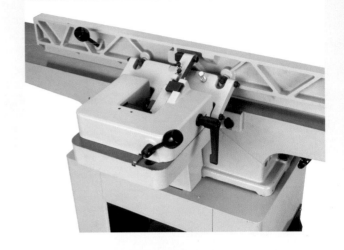

Much of how difficult or easy it is to adjust the fence will depend on the quality of the mating surfaces between the fence and its table extension, as illustrated in the drawing below. If these surfaces are not machined flat and smooth, the fence will never slide properly. You can remove small imperfections with a flat mill file followed by emery cloth, but anything more than that should be brought to the attention of the manufacturer. If you've purchased a used jointer and the surfaces are unsatisfactory, you may need to take your jointer to a local machine shop so they can grind the surfaces flat and smooth. Some manufacturers get around the mating surfaces problem by having the fence slide in and out on a smooth metal rod as shown in the middle photo.

As to the fence lock, many jointers use a common combination of a square T-nut that fits into a groove on the underside of the fence extension. A threaded knob passes through a hole in the fence body and threads into this nut. Since this nut has to slide with the fence, it's also important that it (and the groove it slides in) is smooth and flat.

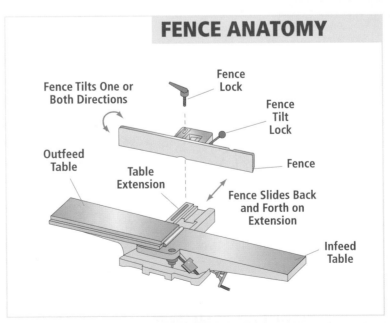

FENCE ANATOMY

Fence Tilts One or Both Directions

Fence Lock

Fence Tilt Lock

Fence

Outfeed Table

Table Extension

Fence Slides Back and Forth on Extension

Infeed Table

FENCE TILT

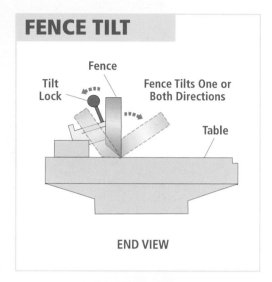

Fence

Tilt Lock

Fence Tilts One or Both Directions

Table

END VIEW

Fence tilt

All jointer fences should be able to tilt so you can make angled cuts: bevels, chamfers, etc. Look for built-in stops that set the fence at 90 and 45 degrees and are easily adjustable. Here again, make sure the locking system is positive and easy to use. You'll find that many jointer fences tilt only one way—that is, they typically tilt away from the table. A quality jointer will always feature a fence that tilts both ways, as illustrated in the top drawing.

Dust collection

Jointers create a surprisingly large amount of dust and chips. Regardless of the stand chosen, it's important for your long-term respiratory health to capture as much of this as possible. Most closed stands are easily adapted for dust control by covering the chip chute with an adapter like the one shown in the right middle photo.

It is possible to capture dust and chips on an open stand; it just takes a different sort of adapter, as shown in the left middle photo. Small bench-top jointers often have no provision for dust collection. Your best bet here is to build a stand that offers a way to control dust and chips, like the one shown in the bottom photo and described in detail on pages 104–107. With this stand the dust and chips exiting the jointer are directed down into a chip bin by way of a simple baffle attached to the top of the stand.

■ JOINTER RECOMMENDATIONS

To choose a jointer, start by identifying the type of work you do. If you work primarily with short stock and won't be working the machine very hard, a bench-top jointer will do the job (top photo). For the more serious wood-worker who is working with longer and wider stock, you'll want to purchase a stationary jointer—either a 6" or an 8" model (middle photo). If you've got the room in the shop, we recommend buying an 8" jointer if you can afford it. We realize that they're quite a bit more expensive, but we can't tell you how many woodworkers we know that purchased a 6" jointer and then realized they'd have better off buying the larger 8" version. We also recommend buying or making a closed base. Enclosing the base is the easiest way to capture and convey dust and chips away to a dust collector. It also keeps the motor, bearings, and belt cleaner so they'll run smoother, longer. If space and budget allow, by all means go with an industrial jointer (bottom photo). You'll enjoy virtually vibration-free smooth cuts in all types and sizes of lumber.

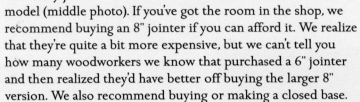

BENCH-TOP JOINTERS

Brand	Max Width	Fence Tilt	Max. Cut	Table Size	Speed	Motor	Weight (lbs.)
Craftsman	$6^1/_8$"	+/– 45	$1/_8$"	$6^1/_8$" × 30"	single	10 amp	106
Delta	6"	0 – 45	$1/_8$"	$6^3/_{16}$" × 30"	variable	10 amp	42
Grizzly	4"	0 – 45	$5/_{64}$"	4" × 23"	single	$1/_2$ hp	28
Palmgren	$6^1/_8$"	+/– 45	$1/_8$"	$6^1/_4$" × $28^1/_2$"	single	1 hp	104
Shop Fox	$6^1/_8$"	0 – 45	$1/_8$"	$6^1/_4$" × $28^1/_2$"	single	2 hp	95
Sunhill	4"	+/– 45	1 mm	$4^1/_4$" × $23^1/_2$"	single	$5/_8$ hp	30
	6"	+/– 45	2 mm	$6^1/_4$" × $27^1/_2$"	single	$1^1/_2$ hp	45

■ JOINTER RECOMMENDATIONS

STATIONARY JOINTERS

Brand/Model	Voltage	Motor	Max. Width	Max. Cut	Bed Length	Weight (lbs.)
Craftsman 40503	110	$3/4$ hp	6"	$1/8$"	46"	182
Craftsman 21703	220	2 hp	$8^{1}/_{8}$"	$1/2$"	71"	420
Delta JT360	110/220	$3/4$ hp	$6^{1}/_{8}$"	$1/8$"	46"	210
Delta 37-350A	110/220	$1^{1}/_{2}$ hp	$8^{1}/_{8}$"	$5/8$"	$72^{3}/_{4}$"	394
General 80-075	110/220	1 hp	6"	$1/2$"	$55^{1}/_{2}$"	235
General 80-200L	220	2 hp	8"	$1/2$"	$74^{7}/_{8}$"	572
Grizzly G0452	110	1 hp	6"	$1/8$"	46"	176
Grizzly G0593	110/220	2 hp	8"	$1/2$"	$75^{1}/_{8}$"	418
Jet JJ-60S	110/220	$3/4$ hp	$6^{1}/_{2}$"	$1/2$"	46"	192
Jet JJ-8CS	220	2 hp	$8^{1}/_{8}$"	$1/2$"	$62^{1}/_{2}$"	398
Powermatic 54A	110/220	1 hp	6"	$1/2$"	66"	332
Powermatic 60B	220	2 hp	$8^{1}/_{8}$"	$1/2$"	$83^{1}/_{8}$"	610
Shop Fox W169	110	1 hp	6"	$1/2$"	47"	300
Shop Fox W1705	220	2 hp	8"	$1/2$"	$70^{1}/_{2}$"	405
Sunhill CT-60L	110/220	1 hp	6"	$1/2$"	52"	220
Sunhill CT-204L	110/220	2 hp	8"	$1/2$"	$74^{7}/_{8}$"	572

INDUSTRIAL JOINTERS

Brand/Model	Voltage	Motor	Max. Width	Max. Cut	Bed Length	Weight (lbs.)
Delta DJ-30	220	3 hp	12"	$3/4$"	84"	706
General 780	220	3 hp	12"	$5/8$"	84"	1,600
General 880	220	5 hp	16"	$5/8$"	96"	1,900
Grizzly G9860	220	3 hp	$11^{3}/_{16}$"	$5/16$"	80"	970
Grizzly G9953	220	5 hp	16"	$5/16$"	$99^{1}/_{4}$"	1,256
Oliver 4255	220	3 hp	12"	$3/4$"	92"	1,550
Oliver 4270	220	5 hp	16"	$3/4$"	102"	1,750
Powermatic 1791241	220	3 hp	$11^{3}/_{4}$"	$3/4$"	84"	880
Powermatic 1791283	220/440	5 hp	16"	$3/4$"	96"	1,400

Planer Basics

Large or small, all planers work similarly. A workpiece placed on the bed of the machine is fed in until the infeed roller grips it. The infeed roller may be rubber, or metal with serrated edges (as shown in the drawing below), to afford a better grip. The infeed roller presses the stock firmly against the planer bed and pushes it forward into the revolving cutterhead, which holds two to four knives.

On heavy-duty planers, there's a metal bar called a chip breaker in front of the cutterhead that breaks off chips lifted by the cutterhead and helps direct them out of the planer. Larger planers often employ a pressure bar after the cutterhead to hold the stock firmly against the bed and prevent it from lifting up after the cut. The outfeed roller (usually rubber) grips the stock and pulls and pushes it out of the planer. Some planers incorporate metal rollers into the bed, set at a slightly higher level, to help reduce friction.

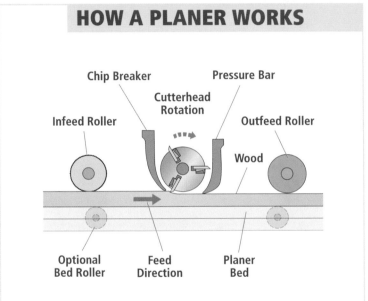

HOW A PLANER WORKS

Chip Breaker

Pressure Bar

Cutterhead Rotation

Infeed Roller

Outfeed Roller

Wood

Optional Bed Roller

Feed Direction

Planer Bed

MOVABLE VS. FIXED CUTTERHEAD

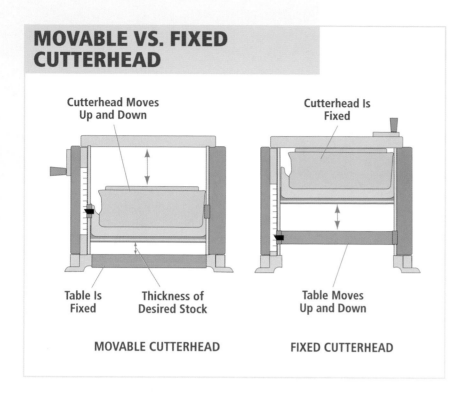

Cutterhead Moves Up and Down

Cutterhead Is Fixed

Table Is Fixed

Thickness of Desired Stock

Table Moves Up and Down

MOVABLE CUTTERHEAD

FIXED CUTTERHEAD

FRAME VS. POST CONSTRUCTION

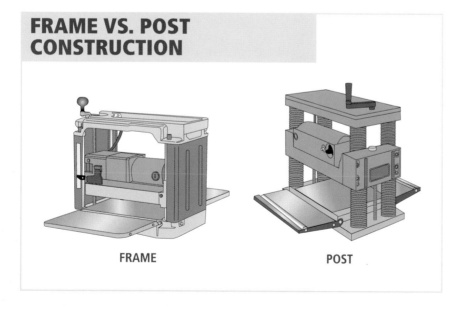

FRAME

POST

Movable versus fixed cutterheads

The amount of wood that's removed is controlled either by lowering or raising the cutterhead, or by raising or lowering the planer bed, as illustrated in the drawing at left. Fixed cutterheads tend to produce smoother cuts because there's no play in the cutterheads, as there can be with a movable cutterhead.

Frame versus post construction

There are two basic designs for planer construction: frame, and post. With the frame design, the actual frame of the planer is used to guide the cutterhead up and down, as illustrated in the bottom drawing. Because of manufacturing tolerances, the cutterhead in a frame-style planer will always have a bit of play and can move during a cut. The exception to this is a frame-style planer with a fixed cutterhead; with this type of planer, the bed moves instead of the cutterhead. On a post-style planer, the cutterhead moves up and down on a set of stout posts; this tends to better support the cutterhead, so play is minimized.

Bench-Top Planers

For decades, home woodworkers could only dream about owning a power planer. That's because power planers were giant beasts weighing upwards of $^1/_2$ ton and costing thousands of dollars. Most required 220 volts to operate and were found only in professional cabinet shops. But that all changed around 1985, when Ryobi introduced the AP-10 portable planer. Diminutive in size (about as large as a suitcase), the AP-10 used a universal motor to make it highly portable—and at around $400, it put this essential workhorse within reach of most hobbyists. Since then virtually every power tool manufacturer has introduced their own version—most can thickness-plane stock up to 6" thick and around 12" to 13" wide.

Although most bench-top planers do an adequate job of creating a smooth finish, they do have some drawbacks. Unlike their heavy-duty cousins (see the opposite page), bench-top planers don't use a serrated metal infeed roller. Instead they use rubber rollers for both infeed and outfeed—the disadvantage here is that they don't afford as good a grip on rough lumber and often skip or stall when dressing rough-sawn stock. They also don't incorporate a chip breaker or pressure bar; so the finish can suffer, and snipe is often present (see pages 66–68 for more on snipe). However, as these tools continue to evolve, manufacturers strive to improve finish, reduce snipe, and add features such as depth stops, accurate depth indicators, and other bells and whistles that make a portable planer a solid investment for the home shop.

BENCH-TOP PLANER ANATOMY

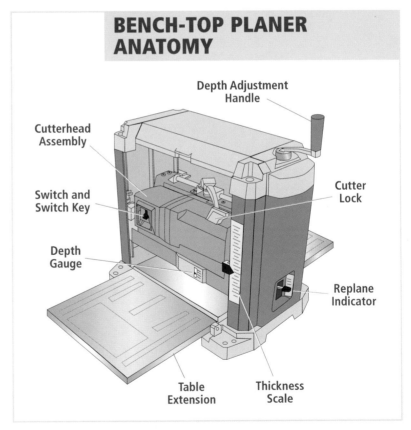

Depth Adjustment Handle

Cutterhead Assembly

Switch and Switch Key

Depth Gauge

Cutter Lock

Replane Indicator

Table Extension

Thickness Scale

Stationary Planers

Many woodworkers get confused when trying to decide between a portable planer and a stationary planer. One big reason is that many of the smaller stationary planers have cutting capabilities similar to a portable planer's, but can easily cost twice as much. If they do the same job, why pay more? Although it may appear that they do the same job, it's like comparing a mini pickup with a full-sized truck: Yes, they can both haul a set amount of weight—but which one will hold up better working day in and day out?

STATIONARY PLANER ANATOMY

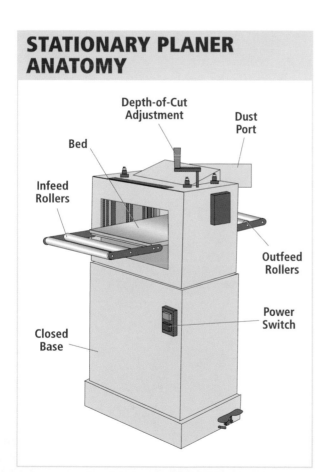

Depth-of-Cut Adjustment

Dust Port

Bed

Infeed Rollers

Outfeed Rollers

Power Switch

Closed Base

The full-sized truck, most likely, because it's built with a heavy workload in mind and engineered for everyday use (and abuse). Stationary planers are similarly designed for heavy-duty use. In addition to using a powerful induction motor instead of the weaker universal motor, the internal parts of a quality stationary planer are beefier, often heavy cast iron and machined to closer tolerances.

Sure, you can surface 100 board feet of white oak with a bench-top planer, but it'll take a long time and will take its toll on the machine. A stationary planer, on the other hand, wouldn't bat an eye at 1000 board feet. Stationary planers, with their serrated metal infeed rollers, are the best choice if you're planning on surfacing rough-sawn lumber. The rubber infeed rollers on portable planers just don't afford as good a grip and often stall, causing burning.

Industrial Planers

Just as with a stationary and an industrial jointer, what sets an industrial planer apart from a stationary planer is capacity and power. A stationary planer typically sports a 3- to 5-horsepower motor and can handle stock that's 6" to 8" thick and 15" to 20" wide. The beefier industrial planers have much larger motors—$7^1/2$ to 15 horsepower—and can tackle 8"- to 9"-thick stock that's 22" to 25" wide. It's important to note that these heavy-duty motors are either 220- or 440-volt and may require three-phase power. Many of these planers have multiple motors: one to drive the cutterhead, one to drive the feed rollers, and if applicable, one to raise and lower the planer bed. Just as with industrial jointers, the average woodworker is hard-pressed to justify the size and cost of one of the mammoths—but they sure are sweet to use. Imagine planing a top for an end table in a single pass!

TYPICAL PLANER CAPACITIES

Trying do decide which planer is best for you? Here's a quick comparison of capacities of the various planer types: bench-top, stationary, and industrial. For detailed specifications, see pages 32–34.

Planer Type	Maximum Depth of Cut	Maximum Width of Cut	Maximum Thickness	Motor Size
Bench-top	$1/8$"	13"	6"	15 amp
Stationary	$1/8$" – $1/4$"	15" – 20"	6" – 8"	3 – 5 hp
Industrial	$1/8$" – $5/16$"	22" – 25"	8" – $9^1/4$"	$7^1/2$ – 15 hp

Planer Features

Bed width

Bed width is an important consideration when you're looking for a planer. It defines the maximum-width board you can pass through the planer, as illustrated in the drawing below and in the photo at left. As we mentioned previously, you can find both bench-top planers and stationary planers with similar capacities. Although the width capacity is similar, the stationary jointer will hold up much better under heavy use. Most serious home woodworkers opt for a 15" stationary planer. Bed length is less important than width since it doesn't limit what you can do with the planer. It really just affects how easy or difficult it is to plane long stock. And since you can use extensions or auxiliary infeed/outfeed support for this, this specification is less important.

Thickness capacity

Thickness capacity is also a concern on planers, but less so, as even small bench-top planers can handle up to 6"-thick stock. Most woodworkers find this more than adequate for their home shop. Larger stationary planers have capacities up to 8", but 6" is also common.

BED WIDTH

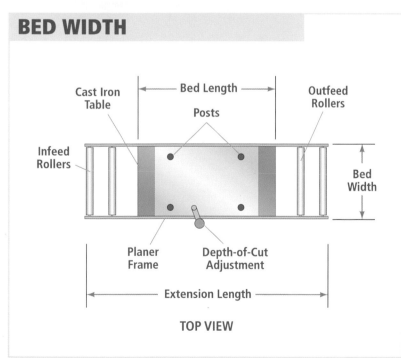

TOP VIEW

Motor size and type

Motor size is fair indication of the planer's power. For universal motors, ignore the horsepower rating and look for the amperage rating of the motor (most bench-top planers use a 15-amp motor), as shown in the top photo. Generally, the higher the amperage, the more powerful the motor. The horsepower ratings on induction motors are fairly accurate, but check the label for the wiring class of the motor—it should at least be a "B" ("F" is superior). Many import motors are not rated at all or have the lowest class ("A"). A motor with a poor wiring class will overheat quickly and need to be replaced.

Stands

Just as with jointers, the stand for a planer can have a large impact on its performance. As with jointers, you can choose between open (bottom photo) and closed stands (middle photo). But since dust collection usually isn't an issue here—dust and chips are collected above, near the cutterhead—either type will work. Look for a stand that's both heavy and well constructed, which will help dampen vibration.

PORTABILITY

Bench-top planers are designed to be portable—even though many top the scales at around 100 pounds. How portable the planer is will depend on a few things: the handles, the extensions, and its weight.

Handles. There are two general types of handles for portable planers: those mounted on the front and back, and those mounted on the sides. Front- and back-mounted handles often also serve as rollers to make it easy to pass lumber from the outfeed back to the infeed table after it has been planed, as shown in the top left photo. We prefer side-mounted handles like those shown in the top right photo, as we find that it's easier to lift and carry a planer from the side.

Table extensions. Most portable power planers come with a set of extension tables to better support the stock. Tables that fold up (like those in the bottom left photo) make it easy to transport a planer, versus extensions that bolt or screw to the planer.

Wheeled stand. If portability is an issue with a stationary planer, choose a stand with built-in wheels that lock, like those shown in the bottom right photo. For the utmost in stability, make sure that all of the wheels lock, and not just one pair.

Planer bed and extensions

Another important planer feature, and one that's often overlooked, is the type of bed and extensions that come standard with a planer. As for the bed, it may be flat or have built-in rollers.

PLANER BEDS. There are advantages and disadvantages to both types of planer beds: flat and with rollers. Flat beds (top left photo) tend to reduce snipe (see page 66) but can make it difficult to pass lumber through the planer. A planer with rollers built into its bed (bottom left photo) reduces friction, so it's easy to pass lumber through the planer. On the downside, bed rollers tend to increase the likelihood of snipe.

EXTENSIONS. Extensions can be stamped metal, cast iron, or rollers. Regardless of the extension type you choose, just make sure that they are adjustable.

Stamped metal. Most portable power planers employ stamped-metal extensions to keep their weight down. They work well, but some aren't adjustable.

Rollers. Roller extensions are an excellent choice, as they reduce friction and offer reasonable support. And most roller extensions are easily adjustable.

Cast iron. Cast extensions offer the best support, but at a price. The friction they generate can make it difficult to pass stock through the planer.

Changing knives

Just as on a jointer, changing knives on a planer can be a hassle. With this in mind, it's worth the time to investigate the knife-changing procedure for the planer(s) you have in mind. One of the biggest challenges to changing planer knives is access. Most portable planers are pretty tight (top photo), while the larger stationary and industrial planers offer better access; see below.

PORTABLE PLANERS. Some of the bench-top planer manufactures have gone to double-sided disposable knives that can be flipped when one side dulls, and thrown away when both dull, as shown in the top photo. Replacement blades are fairly inexpensive and often very easy to replace.

STATIONARY PLANERS. The knives in stationary planers are often spring-loaded and are held in place with bolts and gibs, as shown in the middle photo. Space is still pretty tight here, and the knives are best changed with the aid of a magnetic-setting jig (see pages 159–160).

INDUSTRIAL PLANERS. Since industrial planers are designed to plow through hundreds of board feet per day, the knives need regular sharpening. With this in mind, the manufacturers provide excellent access to the knives—an example of this is shown in the bottom photo.

Dust collection

If you've ever operated a planer without any kind of chip and dust collection, you know how much waste a planer can generate. Virtually all planers now come with the ability to collect chips and dust. Some makers include a dust port with the planer, which you hook up to your shop vacuum or dust collector; others sell the port as an accessory.

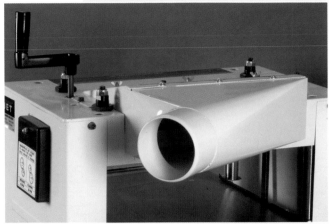

There are two basic styles of dust ports that differ in where they collect dust and chips: side or center. With a side dust port (top photo), your shop vacuum or dust collector has to pull chips all the way from the far end of the cutterhead. A better port is the centered type, shown in the middle photo. Here the vacuum or collector pulls chips and dust an equal distance from the cutterhead and tends to be more efficient than the side-mount variety.

DIGITAL DEPTH SCALE

The Powermatic model 15S deluxe planer sports a digital depth scale that takes all the guesswork out of thickness-planing. It features two modes: absolute and relative. In absolute mode, board thickness is determined by the distance from the table to the cutterhead—and so will represent the thickness of your board. In relative mode, the table can be "zeroed" out at any position and will indicate not the thickness of the board, but how much material will be removed.

PLANER/MOLDERS

If you've always wanted a shaper but couldn't justify the shop space or the expense, consider buying a planer/molder. These multi-purpose machines combine the functions of a stationary planer and a shaper (or molder). Although not as versatile as a shaper, it can produce an amazing array of molded profiles—everything from crown molding to tongue-and-groove flooring (see the drawing below right).

The way it works is that there's a section in the middle of the cutterhead where you can remove a set of spacers and replace these with molding cutters, as shown in the top photo. (Note that wide cutters require that the knives be removed entirely.) A shop-made bed with guide rails is attached to the bed of the planer, and the stock is fed through. Alternatively, some tool makers include a guide rail system, or you can purchase it separately. (For more on using a planer/molder, see pages 96–97.)

CUTTER PROFILE	CUTTER PROFILE
Crown	Ogee Window Stop
Crown	Picture Frame
Crown	Picture Frame
Chair Rail	Picture Frame
Chair Rail	Picture Frame
Bed	Tongue and Groove
Astragal	Dado/Rabbet/Back Relief
Astragal	Cove
Five Bead	Quarter Round
Base Shoe	Casing
1/4" and 1/2" Quarter Round	Casing
Three Bead	Chair Rail
Flute	Crown
Casing	Base
Crown	Crown

■ PLANER RECOMMENDATIONS

Choosing a planer is a bit more complicated than selecting a jointer, as there are more choices involved. The first step again is looking at what type of work you expect to do. If you're planning on surfacing rough-sawn lumber, go with a stationary planer and make sure it has a serrated-metal infeed roller. Also, if your woodworking requires a lot of planing, you'll be better served with a stationary planer. If you're going to purchase a larger machine, consider investing in at least a 15" planer with a large dust collection port (5" to 6" in diameter) and a closed base.

Bench-top

If you work primarily with surfaced wood, and your woodworking is limited to nights and weekends (like most of us), a quality bench-top planer will get the job done. Look for a model with adjustable infeed/outfeed tables, easy-to-adjust controls, and disposable knives that are simple to change or replace. Also, new advancements in planer design (like a cutterhead lock) have greatly reduced snipe—consider this when you shop.

BENCH-TOP PLANERS

Brand/Model	Motor	Max. Width	Max. Thickness	Max. Cut	Cutterhead Speed (rpm)	Weight (lbs.)
Craftsman 21743	15 amp	13"	6"	$1/8$"	8,000	105
Delta 22-580	15 amp	13"	$6^{1}/_{2}$"	$1/8$"	10,000	97
Dewalt DW735	15 amp	13"	6"	$1/8$"	10,000	92
Grizzly G8794	15 amp	$12^{1}/_{2}$"	6"	$1/8$"	8,450	75
Hitachi P13F	15 amp	13"	6"	$1/8$"	8,000	101
Jet JWP-13DX	15 amp	13"	6"	$1/8$"	8,000	77
Palmgren 84113	15 amp	13"	6"	$1/8$"	8,000	106
Rigid TP1300LS	15 amp	13"	6"	$1/8$"	9,000	85
Ryobi AP1301	15 amp	13"	6"	$1/8$"	10,000	54

■ PLANER RECOMMENDATIONS

STATIONARY PLANERS

Brand/Model	Voltage	Motor	Max. Width	Max. Thickness	Max. Cut	Cutterhead Speed (rpm)	Weight (lbs.)
Craftsman 21704	220	3 hp	20"	8"	$1/4$"	20,000	780
Delta DC-380	220	3 hp	15"	$6^1/4$"	$1/8$"	5,000	340
Delta DC-580	220	5 hp	20"	$8^5/8$"	$1/8$"	5,000	840
General 30-125	220	3 hp	$14^7/8$"	6"	$1/8$"	5,000	539
General 30-300	220	3 hp	20"	8"	$1/8$"	5,000	880
Grizzly G0453	220	3 hp	15"	8"	$1/8$"	5,000	661
Grizzly G0454	220	5 hp	20"	8"	$1/8$"	5,000	860
Jet JWP-16OS	220	3 hp	16"	6"	$3/16$"	4,500	396
Jet JWP-208	220/440	3/5 hp	20"	8"	$3/32$"	5,000	640
Powermatic 1791209	220	3 hp	$14^5/8$"	6"	$1/8$"	4,500	540
Powermatic 1791297	220	5 hp	20"	8"	$3/32$"	5,000	770
Sunhill CT-38B	220	3 hp	15"	6"	$1/8$"	5,000	500
Sunhill CT-508	220	5 hp	20"	8"	$1/4$"	5,000	925

■ PLANER RECOMMENDATIONS

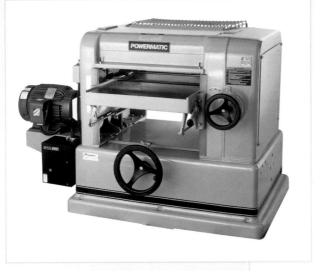

INDUSTRIAL PLANERS

Brand/Model	Voltage	Motor	Max. Width	Max. Thickness	Max. Cut	Cutterhead Speed (rpm)	Weight (lbs.)
Delta 22-470	220	7$\frac{1}{2}$ hp	24"	8$\frac{5}{8}$"	$\frac{3}{16}$"	5,000	980
General 30-460	220	7$\frac{1}{2}$ hp	24"	8"	$\frac{5}{16}$"	4,800	1,104
Grizzly G9471	220	10 hp	24"	9"	$\frac{1}{8}$"	3,450	1,785
Oliver 4470	220/440	10 hp	25"	9$\frac{1}{4}$"	$\frac{1}{4}$"	4,800	1,837
Powermatic 1791261	220	7$\frac{1}{2}$ hp	22"	9$\frac{1}{4}$"	$\frac{3}{16}$"	4,800	1,350
Powermatic 1791303	220/440	15 hp	25"	9"	$\frac{1}{4}$"	5,000	1,850

JOINTER-PLANERS

A number of space-conscious toolmakers manufacturer combination jointer-planers. Most of these come in an "over and under" configuration, where the jointer on top and the planer below share a common cutterhead. The benefit to a combination machine is that you get two tools in the space of one, so small shops will really benefit from this. The downside to a combination machine is that there's always a certain amount of time required to switch functions between planing and jointing. Also, since the planer is under the jointer, you have to stoop down low to pass stock through the planer. Both of the tools shown here are sold by Laguna Tools (www.lagunatools.com).

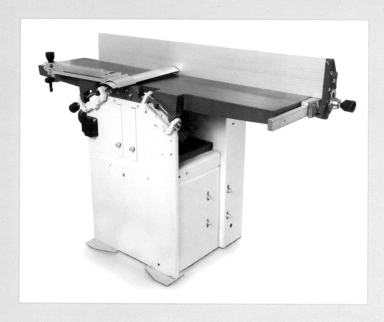

The xsd310 shown in the top photo is a 12" jointer with a 3-hp motor. The table is 55" long and made of stout cast iron. Cutterhead speed is 5,500 rpm, and it takes about 20 seconds to change over to the planing function. The planer can handle stock 12" wide and 9" thick. Its maximum depth of cut is $1/4$", and the feed rate is 19 feet per minute. The cutterhead of the Austrian-made Knapp AD310 jointer-planer shown in the bottom photo is a little over 12" wide. The length of the jointer is 67" and with two cast-iron extensions reaches to 106".

2 Jointer and Planer Accessories

Most power tools have a gaggle of accessories that you can buy for them—jointers and planers have just a few. Much of this has to do with the simplicity of both tools and with the fact that each tool is primarily designed to do a single task, and to do it well. In this chapter, we'll start with jointer accessories: push blocks, stands, knives, and knife-setting jigs. For the planer, accessories include replacement blades, replacement cutterheads, stands, and blade-setting and blade-sharpening jigs. For both tools there are also support stands, motor accessories, and tool-tuning accessories.

The majority of the accessories for jointers and planers are related to the cutterheads: replacement knives, new spiral cutterheads, and alignment aids like dial indicators and magnetic positioning jigs.

Jointer Accessories

Besides the pivoting guard that comes standard on every jointer, a push block is the next most important safety device. Savvy manufacturers are now including a set with every jointer—that's because they know all too well how dangerous an exposed cutterhead can be. It's just a lot safer to run a board over a cutterhead with a safety barrier (the push block) between your hand and the workpiece. Let's face it: Accidents do happen in the shop. One way to prevent a nasty one with a jointer is to use a push block whenever possible.

Commercial push blocks

Commercially made push blocks come in a variety of shapes and sizes. The most common type resembles a grout float used for tile work. This style of push block has a rubber cushion on the bottom and does not have a lip (top photo). The gripping power is provided by the rubber face and can slip if it's not kept clean—it's a good idea to give this type of push block a quick shot of compressed air before each use. Over time, sawdust can build up, and the rubber face should be cleaned with a mild detergent solution.

Shop-made push blocks

The style of push block that we prefer for use on the jointer is the type that has a lip like the one shown in the middle photo. The lip fits over the edge of the workpiece and provides a more positive grip. We've had no-lip push blocks slip before, and we didn't care for the experience at all. The push block shown here is easy to make and will serve you well for years. See pages 102–103 for directions on how to make it.

Grout float push blocks

If you've ever done any tile work and have a grout float lying around (bottom photo), you can press it into service as a push block. Like most commercially available push blocks, a grout float doesn't have a lip, and works well for applying pressure to the workpiece as it passes over the cutterhead. Make sure to use the older-style floats that sport a black rubber cushion. Newer floats tend to come with a hard rubber surface that's very slick and won't grip the workpiece safely.

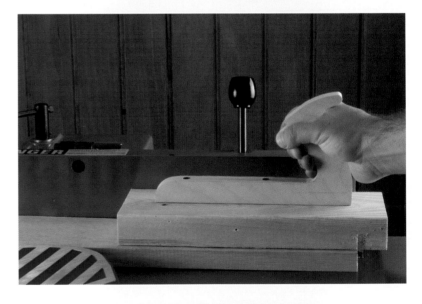

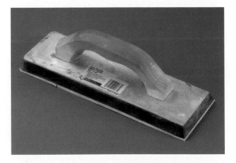

Commercial stands

The base or stand of a jointer can have a big impact on the jointer's performance. The heavier it is, and the sturdier the construction, the better it can dampen vibration. The open base stand shown in the top photo is our last choice for a stand, for a couple of reasons. First, although it's fairly sturdy, it doesn't weigh much. But more important, this type of stand does not lend itself well to dust collection. A sturdy, closed base stand provides both a solid foundation for the jointer and a quick and easy way to control and convey dust and chips. To hook the jointer up to a dust collector, all you need to do is attach a pickup to the dust chute and connect this via flexible hose to your collector. An added benefit of a closed base is that it shields the motor from collecting shop dust. Fine dust like this can penetrate into the bearings and coat the windings—both of which can shorten the life of the motor.

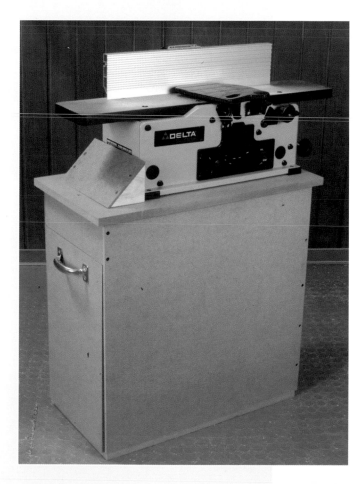

Shop-made stands

An alternative to buying a closed base stand is to build one yourself. The shop-made stand shown in the bottom photo is built using 3/4" MDF (medium-density fiberboard). Since this material is dense and heavy (about 100 pounds per sheet) and it uses most of a sheet, it does a good job of dampening vibration. This stand also features a pullout chip bin that contains and collects chips for removal. (For step-by-step instructions on how to make this stand, see pages 104–107.)

Jointer Knives

Jointer knives come in three basic flavors: high-speed steel, solid carbide, and carbide-tipped.

High-speed steel

Most jointers come standard with a set of HSS (high-speed steel) knives, as shown in the top photo. These knives will perform admirably in most shop situations, can be resharpened, and will last for years. Jointer knives are available in a wide variety of widths and lengths, with or without mounting holes or slots. When you go to purchase a replacement knife (or another set), it's best to buy from the original manufacturer to ensure that it'll fit properly in your jointer.

Solid carbide

Solid carbide knives are expensive—roughly 10 times more than HSS knives—so they're not for everyone. As with any carbide tool, their biggest advantage is that they stay sharp longer. And since the entire knife is carbide (middle photo), they can be resharpened many more times than a carbide-tipped knife (see below). If you're working with a lot of highly abrasive woods (like teak, ebony, or osage orange), a set of solid carbide knives may be worth the investment. Otherwise, we recommend sticking with HSS or carbide-tipped knives.

Carbide-tipped

For a longer-lasting edge, you might want to consider a set of carbide-tipped knives. This type of knife has a high-speed steel body with a length of carbide permanently bonded to the tip, as illustrated in the bottom drawing. This style of knife is less brittle than a solid carbide knife and is less expensive. Carbide-tipped knives typically run 3 to 4 times the cost of HSS knives. Although they do hold an edge longer, they nick more easily and are much more costly to have sharpened.

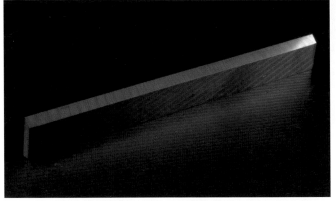

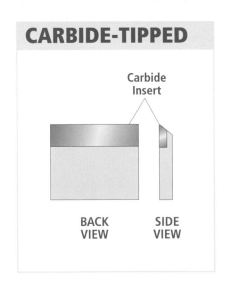

CARBIDE-TIPPED

Carbide Insert

BACK VIEW

SIDE VIEW

Spiral HSS knives

Some blade and cutterhead manufacturers have recently incorporated into their products the age-old technique of skewing a blade to produce a cleaner, shearing cut. Variations include spiral knives and spiral and helical cutterheads (see below). With a HSS spiral cutterhead, the knives wrap around the cutterhead in a spiral, as shown in the top photo. The end result is much smoother cuts than with straight knives—this is especially true when working on woods with highly figured grain.

Carbide spiral cutterhead

Since carbide is brittle and doesn't bend without breaking, a different technique was needed to create a spiral cutterhead with carbide knives. The solution was to machine the blade into smaller tabs that could then flex around the cutterhead, as shown in the middle photo. The carbide holds up better than HSS but doesn't produce as smooth a finish.

Carbide helical cutterhead

The ultimate in spiral cutterheads is a helical cutterhead with individual inserts, as shown in the bottom photo. This type of cutterhead offers a number of advantages. First, each insert is sharpened on all four edges. If it dulls, simply remove, rotate, and secure it for a fresh edge. Second, if you nick your cutterhead, you can locate the nicked inserts and rotate them instead of removing, sharpening, and reinstalling all the knives. The drawback? The cost—a typical 8" helical spiral cutterhead runs anywhere from $400 to $500.

Jointer Knife-Setting Jigs

Jointer knives have a well-deserved reputation for being a hassle to adjust. Much has to do with how they're held in place with gibs (for more on this, see pages 144–151).

Dial indicator

Our favorite tool for adjusting jointer knives is a dial indicator like the one shown in the photo below. Fitted with a magnetic base that holds it securely to your jointer bed, it lets you make knife-height measurements in increments of a thousandth of an inch. This super-accurate tool is the ultimate way to precisely set the height of the knives (for detailed instructions on using a dial indicator, see pages 148–149).

Magnetic alignment jig

Since changing and adjusting jointer knives can be challenging, a number of tool accessory manufacturers have come up with jigs to make the job easier. The most common of these is a magnetic knife-setting jig, like the one shown in the photo below. This style of jig uses two sets of powerful magnets: one to attach to the jointer bed, and the other to hold the knives in perfect position so that you can tighten the mounting bolts or screws. Most of these will work on jointers with knives up to 8" wide, regardless of the diameter of the cutterhead.

Planer Accessories

The same features that describe a well-made jointer stand—heavy and sturdy—apply to planer stands. But unlike jointer stands, where a closed base is best, planers will work equally well with an open or a closed base. That's because dust and chip collection isn't an issue for the stand: Dust and chips are collected from planers from above. In most cases a dust port or hood is attached directly to or over the planer head and is then connected to a dust collector via a flexible hose. With this in mind, selecting an open versus closed base is really a matter of personal preference. For the most part, woodworkers that have other machines with closed bases tend to stick with closed bases, more for looks than anything else. Here again, the advantage that an open base has is that it often affords more storage space— you could easily add a lower shelf to the shop-made stand shown below.

Commercial stands

Most tool manufacturers offer both closed (top photo) and open (middle photo) bases for their tools. Closed bases often weigh more than the equivalent open stand and can therefore dampen vibration better.

Shop-made stand

Shop-made stands are an alternative to buying one. If you decide to build one, stick with heavy materials (like MDF) and use sturdy construction— like the dovetailed base shown here. Because of its open base style, you can add a shelf below for storage. This stand also features table extensions to help support long stock and prevent snipe. For step-by-step directions on how to build this planer stand, see pages 110–115.

Replacement knives

As with a jointer, you'll find a wide variety of replacement knives available for your planer. These include high-speed steel (HSS), carbide-tipped, and solid carbide, as shown in the top photo. The average woodworker generally has a tough time justifying the higher cost of carbide blades. Solid carbide knives can cost anywhere from 8 to 12 times the cost of high-speed steel. In between are carbide-tipped knives, which typically cost 3 to 4 times more than high-speed steel.

Replacement cutterhead

If you want to step up from a standard cutterhead to a spiral cutterhead with high-speed steel knives, carbide blades, or individual inserts (see the sidebar below), you'll have to replace the cutterhead as shown in the photo at right. For step-by-step instructions on installing a spiral cutterhead, see pages 152–153.

HELICAL AND SPIRAL CUTTERHEADS

Spiral cutterheads for planers are becoming so popular that many tool manufacturers are now offering versions of their standard planers with the upgraded spiral cutterhead already installed. Yes, these cost hundreds of dollars more, but this saves you the hassle of installing one, plus it offers all the benefits of spiral cutting.

By their design, all spiral cutterheads produce a shearing cut in lieu of the standard chopping cut produced by a standard cutterhead with straight knives. And a shearing cut produces a smoother finish—especially on highly figured woods. If you choose a helical spiral cutterhead with individual inserts, you'll enjoy the ease of replacement—you can even replace just a single insert if it gets nicked, instead of having to replace an entire knife or set of knives.

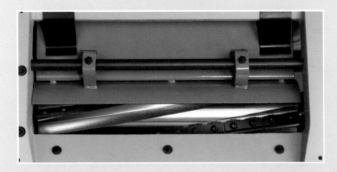

Planer Knife-Setting Jigs

Setting planer knives can be as tricky as setting and adjusting jointer knives, so manufacturers have developed a number of alignment aids and positioning jigs.

Blade height gauge

The simplest planer knife alignment aid is a height gauge that straddles the knife and has a centered tab on its underside, as shown in the top photo. The knife is raised until it butts up against the tab and then is tightened. Since you have to hold the gauge in one hand, you have to position and tighten the knife with the other. And unless you have three arms, this is almost impossible to do.

Magnetic alignment jigs

A better solution is to use one of the many magnetic knife-setting jigs available; see below. These jigs all feature magnets to hold the knife in place, freeing up your hands to adjust and lock the knife in place. It's important to purchase a knife-setting jig that's designed for the diameter of your cutterhead.

Large magnetic jig. This type of jig has pairs of powerful magnets set into a metal head that fits the curve of the cutterhead. A third magnet in the jig holds the knife in position while you tighten the gib screws or bolts.

Adjustable magnetic jig. This nifty knife-setting jig manufactured by General tools (www.general.ca.) is sort of a hybrid of a dial indicator and a magnetic knife-setting jig. It uses magnets to hold the knife in place but lets you adjust knife position with precision.

Small magnetic jig. On this smaller, less expensive cousin of the large magnetic jig, the magnets are set into a plastic head. This dainty jig is used to adjust knives on portable planers—it's not large enough for a stationary planer.

Knife-Sharpening Jigs

The knives in your planer or jointer will eventually dull and need to be resharpened. There are two basic methods for handling this task. If the knives are in reasonable shape (no nicks or severely blunted edges), it may be possible to touch them up in place with a honing stone (see below). Please note that honing doesn't replace sharpening; it simply lengthens the time required between sharpenings. To sharpen jointer or planer knives, you'll first need to remove them. And unless you've got a specialty sharpening system (like the Tormek system shown below), you'll need to drop off your planer knives at a sharpening service. Ask your woodworking buddies or the local guild for recommendations for a sharpening service if you haven't used one before.

Honing stone

There are a couple honing stones available for quickly bringing up a fresh edge on your jointer or planer knives. The one shown in the top photo has two different-shaped stones embedded in a plastic holder. The square stone is used to lap the back of the knife, and the other stone is beveled to match the angle of the knives. When using one of these, make sure the knives are clean and the machine is unplugged prior to sharpening.

Tormek system

The Tormek system (www.tormek.com) is a water-cooled grinding unit that allows for either fast or slow cutting action on the same wheel (middle photo). Since it's water-cooled, there's no risk of overheating a knife or blade, causing it to lose its temper. But what really makes the Tormek system unique are the numerous holding jigs available (bottom photo) that guarantee precise angles coupled with repeatable grinds. The big advantage to this is that once you've ground the tool to the exact angle and shape, you only have to remove a tiny bit of material on subsequent sharpenings. This means that the knives or blades will last longer.

The only drawback to this system is its cost. The system plus the jointer/planer knife-sharpening jig (bottom photo) will run you over $500. Granted, you can get a lot of knives sharpened for that, but if you do invest in one of these, you'll find that you'll use it for all your tools. The bottom line is that this is the only sharpening system we've seen for home woodworkers that can handle long jointer and planer knives.

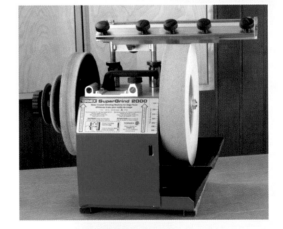

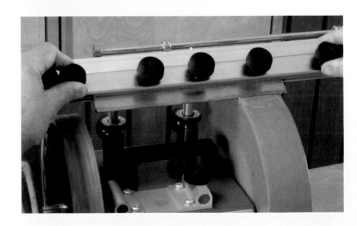

Support Stands

If you don't fully support a workpiece as it passes into and out of a jointer or planer, the workpiece can tilt or pivot up or down into a cutterhead, gouging its ends. One way to help prevent this from happening is to fully support the workpiece with an infeed and/or outfeed support stand.

Roller stands

The most common type of support available, a roller stand like the one shown in the top photo, can be purchased for under $40. They are adjustable in height over a fairly wide range and can be used to support stock when operating a wide variety of tools.

Non-roller stand

A typical roller stand does a fair job of supporting a workpiece, but it does have a couple of inherent design flaws. First, if the roller isn't absolutely parallel to the back edge of the tool, the roller will tend to move the workpiece in the direction the roller is facing. This means if it's not dead-on, it'll cause the workpiece to skew to one side or the other. Second, a workpiece fed onto a roller will tend to roll away unassisted. Both problems are eliminated by replacing the roller with a pair of low-friction skids (middle photo). That's exactly what the folks at Triton have done (www.triton.net.au). To make their stand even better, the head of their stand has a built-in clamp that swivels so it can be used for much more than outfeed support. And like all quality stands, the Triton folds up for compact storage.

Shop-made stand

We designed a version of the non-roller-type support that you can build yourself (see the bottom photo). For complete directions on how to make this infeed/outfeed support, see pages 116–121.

Motor Accessories

Vibration in a power tool is never good. Not only will it affect the performance of the tool, it'll also shorten its life. Vibration tends to loosen parts that should be tight, and the ensuing wear created by parts rubbing together can often lead to breakdown. Vibration works its way through all parts of a planer or jointer; when it reaches the cutterhead, it can cause it to chatter, resulting in a rough or scalloped cut. Besides mounting your jointer or planer to a solid, heavy stand and keeping it properly maintained (periodic lubrication and inspection—see Chapter 6), you can also help reduce vibration with a couple of motor upgrades: machined pulleys and interlocking anti-vibration belts.

Machined pulleys

The pulleys that come standard on most power tools are cast. These tend be rough and unbalanced. And an unbalanced pulley will vibrate. Machined pulleys (middle photo) are available from a number of mail-order woodworking suppliers. If you can't find the size you need, a local machine shop should be able to turn a set for you for a modest fee. Just be sure to take your original pulleys with you to the shop so they can size the machined ones accordingly.

Anti-vibration belts

There are two basic types of belts that drive most stationary power tools: V-belts and the interlocking style. V-belts come in a variety of thickness to fit different pulleys. They also come in various diameters to span a wide range of distances between pulleys. You can find V-belts of various sizes at any automotive store (or you may have to special-order it from the manufacturer). Take your old belt with you to make sure that you get the right size replacement.

A better belt alternative is the interlocking link belt shown in the bottom photo. Unlike a standard V-belt that takes the shape of the tool's pulleys, the individual links of the interlocking belt keep it flexible for life. And a flexible belt greatly reduces the transfer of vibration. If you've got a number of belt-driven machines in your shop, consider purchasing a couple feet of interlocking belt, as the links can be interlocked to form any size belt you need—sort of a "universal" belt.

Tune-Up Accessories

In addition to the specialty jigs for maintaining and tuning jointers and planers, there are a couple other accessories that you may find handy. These include straightedges, dial calipers, and alignment blocks.

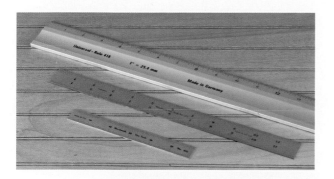

Straightedges

Woodworkers can choose from a wide variety of straightedges, made of either metal or wood (top photo). We prefer metal because its thinness reduces problems with parallax associated with the thicker wooden rules. In our shop we have a 6", 12", 18", and 1-meter metal rule. The 18" length is especially handy for checking a planer bed for flatness.

Dial calipers

A dial caliper is one of the most accurate ways to precisely measure the thickness of stock—and they're incredibly easy to use (middle photo). Just slide open the jaws, insert the workpiece, and slide the jaws tightly closed. Make sure the jaws are in complete contact with the workpiece to get the most accurate reading. You'll find dial calipers with metal or plastic bodies. Even though the metal bodies are typically more accurate, we prefer the plastic bodies for a couple of reasons. First, they're less likely to mar the wood. And second, they're less expensive. We've found the plastic dial calipers to be more than accurate for everyday use. When shopping for a dial caliper, look for one that's calibrated in both 100ths and 64ths of an inch. Be careful: Many of these only read in 100ths of an inch; even though there's a conversion chart on the caliper or case, it's a hassle to use. Stick with a caliper with 64ths clearly labeled on the dial face.

Machined alignment blocks

To accurately align the guide feed and pressure rollers on a stationary planer, you need an accurate alignment block. Although you can make these out of wood, metal blocks (bottom photo) will stay a lot more accurate over time. Some tool makers offer these for their specific machines.

3 Basic Jointer and Planer Techniques

Proper jointing and planing techniques create the foundation for your projects by creating square stock. Without these fundamental building blocks, a project is doomed to turn out less than satisfactory. In this chapter, we'll cover how to set up your jointer, then take you through the techniques for edge- and face-jointing—everything from proper grain direction to types of push blocks and when to use them. Then it's on to planer setup and basic techniques, including ways to deal with warp and snipe. This is followed by our recommended sequence for squaring up stock. If you religiously follow this sequence (and your tools are properly adjusted), you'll end up with square, flat stock—a real pleasure to work with.

A planer is the perfect tool for creating uniform parallel edges or faces. But for this to happen, one face must first be trued with the jointer.

Jointer Setup

If you ever watch a pro woodworker in action, you'll often catch the person doing a quick "pre-flight" check on a tool before using it. Sometimes this checkup is so fast it's hardly notice-able, but it's there. It sort of like what many people do when they go to drive their car. Often, it's not even a conscious thing—they glance at the car's tires as they open the car door. As they sit down, they note that all the windows are intact. They buckle up and turn on the ignition. As they put the car in gear, they glance at the fuel gauge. All of this takes mere seconds. That's the same sort of routine that you should work toward for the jointer. The big things to keep an eye on are the fence, the depth of cut, and the guard.

Fence position

The first step is to adjust the position of the jointer fence. Loosen the fence lock, slide the fence into the desired position, and retighten the lock as shown in the top photo. It's a good idea to routinely move the fence over the entire width of the table so that the full width of the knives gets used. If you don't, and you do a lot of edge-jointing, the area adjacent to the fence will get dull. Then when you go to face-joint a workpiece, you'll get an uneven cut.

Fence squareness

Many woodworkers carry a small engineer's square in their apron. Fences can and will go out of square with use. That's why it's important to routinely check it for square. Just butt an engineer's square against the fence and look for any gaps between the blade body and the fence and table. If you see any, loosen the fence lock and adjust the fence so it's square, as shown in the middle photo.

Fence tilt

If you're going to be beveling or chamfering, you'll want to adjust the fence now to the desired angle. Loosen the fence-tilt lock and adjust the fence as shown in the bottom photo. (For more on cutting bevels and chamfers, see Chapter 4.)

Depth of cut

The next thing to do is to set the depth of cut, as shown in the top photo. Start by loosening the infeed table lock, and then turn the handwheel or adjust the lever to move the infeed table up or down as desired (see your owner's manual for the maximum recommended cut). Note that though most jointers will have a depth-of-cut gauge, they only serve as a rough estimate of how much stock will be removed. Once the depth is set, retighten the lock.

Guard position

The final step before jointing is to check to make sure that the guard is set up and functioning properly. First, check that the guard swings easily out of the way, yet still springs back to touch the fence—and that no portion of the knives is exposed. If you can see knives—stop and adjust the guard, replace the spring, or do what's necessary to correct this dangerous fault. It's also a good idea to periodically loosen the fence lock and slide the fence to its limits to make sure the gaurd stays in contact with the fence as shown in the middle photo.

JOINTER SAFETY CHART

1. Always wear eye protection.

2. Do not wear loose clothing, long sleeves, or jewelry when operating a jointer.

3. Guards should be in place and used at all times.

4. Make sure any exposed cutterhead behind the fence is guarded, especially when jointing near the edge.

5. Never exceed the maximum depth of cut.

6. Always use hold-downs or push blocks when jointing material narrower than 3".

7. Always keep hands and fingers away from the cutterhead.

8. Make all adjustments and repairs with the power off.

9. Keep the work area clean.

10. Never leave a jointer running unattended; always turn it off before stepping away.

11. Never joint any material shorter than 8".

12. Avoid jointing thin material that can get caught under the guard.

13. Jointer blades are extremely sharp; use caution when cleaning or changing them.

14. Whenever possible, use some form of chip and dust collection.

15. Use suitable support for long or heavy workpieces.

Edge-Jointing

Edge-jointing is one of the most common operations performed on the jointer. It can both clean up and straighten edges with a single pass, or multiple passes.

Proper technique

To create smooth, straight edges when edge-jointing, it's important that you understand proper jointing technique. At the start of the cut, pressure is applied to the front end of the work-piece as it makes contact with the cutterhead. As you push the workpiece past the cutterhead, pressure is still applied to the infeed table but is quickly transferred to the outfeed table, as illustrated in the top drawing. Then the majority of the pressure is applied to the outfeed table side as the cut is finished.

Grain direction

Regardless of the jointing operation, to get the smoothest cut, you need to take into account the grain direction of the workpiece. For the best overall cut, the grain should slope down and away from the cutterhead, as shown in the bottom drawing. In a perfect world this isn't always possible. All woodworkers know that grain can switch direction in a piece—often multiple times. In cases like this, try to joint the piece so the majority of the grain is sloping down and away—and take a very light cut.

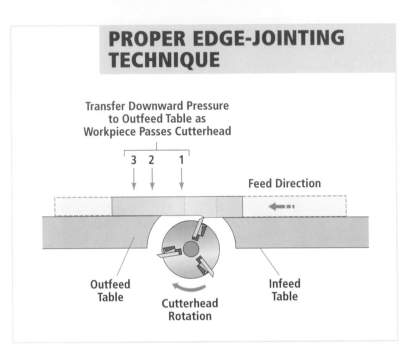

PROPER EDGE-JOINTING TECHNIQUE

Transfer Downward Pressure to Outfeed Table as Workpiece Passes Cutterhead

3 2 1

Feed Direction

Outfeed Table

Infeed Table

Cutterhead Rotation

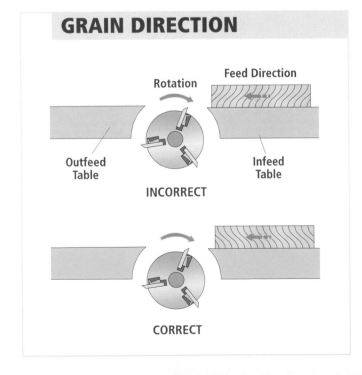

GRAIN DIRECTION

Rotation

Feed Direction

Outfeed Table

Infeed Table

INCORRECT

CORRECT

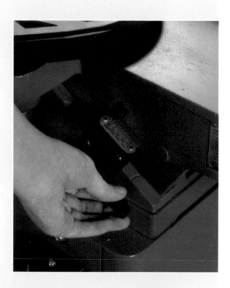

Adjust depth of cut

If you haven't already adjusted the depth of cut per your "pre-flight" check (see pages 52–53), do so now. Loosen the infeed table lock, and then turn the handwheel and lock the table in place (as shown in the top photo) or adjust the lever to move the infeed table up or down as desired (see your owner's manual for the maximum recommended cut). Note that although most jointers have a depth-of-cut gauge, they only serve as a rough estimate of how much stock will be removed. Once the depth is set, retighten the table lock.

Check the fence

Part of your "pre-flight" check should also be checking the fence for square. If you haven't already done this, do so now as shown in the middle photo.

Use the proper stance

Edge-jointing can be quite fatiguing if you don't use the proper stance and develop a natural rhythm—especially if you're edge-jointing a lot of boards. A wide stance provides a stable base and allows you to shift your weight from your back leg to your front leg as the workpiece passes over the cutterhead, as shown in the bottom photo. If the workpiece isn't long, you should be able to joint the entire edge in a single pass without changing your stance. As long as you have a parts cart (see pages 122–125) within reach, you can joint all your edges without moving.

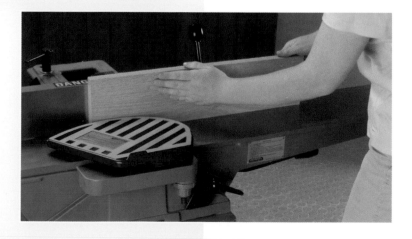

Start the cut

Edge-jointing is a fairly straightforward operation, as long as you follow a couple of simple rules. First, make sure to press the workpiece firmly into the side of the fence at all times in order to achieve a perpendicular cut. Second, position the workpiece a few inches away from the cutterhead and slowly feed the workpiece past the guard, as shown in the top photo. As the workpiece crosses the cutterhead, shift your weight to the outfeed table.

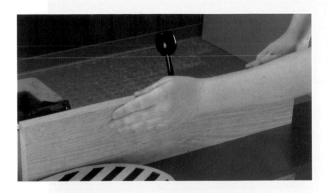

Finish the cut

It's a common misconception of many woodworkers that you should press down heavily on the infeed table. Although you should press down some here, the bulk of the pressure should always be on the outfeed. That's why it's important to shift your weight to the outfeed side as soon as the workpiece passes the cutterhead, as shown in the photo at right.

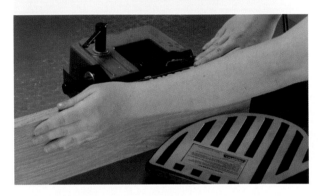

DEALING WITH BOWED STOCK

Stock that's bowed along its length (as shown in the drawing at right) can be a challenge to edge-joint, as there are only two contact points—one at each end of the board. There are two common methods to deal with this. With the first method, you nibble the high points off the ends by passing them repeatedly over the cutterhead to create a straighter edge. The second method is useful if you need shorter pieces; by cutting the board into smaller sections, you dramatically reduce the bow.

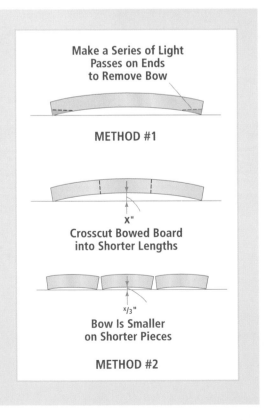

Make a Series of Light Passes on Ends to Remove Bow

METHOD #1

x"

Crosscut Bowed Board into Shorter Lengths

x/3"

Bow Is Smaller on Shorter Pieces

METHOD #2

AUXILIARY FENCES FOR EDGE-JOINTING

There are a couple of auxiliary fences that you may find helpful when edge-jointing challenging pieces, especially those that are wide and/or have grain that's highly figured or squirrelly: a tall fence and a skewed fence.

Tall fence. The challenge with edge-jointing wide boards is that the fence is often not tall enough to fully support the workpiece and the workpiece ends up tilting or wobbling, producing an uneven edge. The solution to this problem is a tall fence like that shown in the drawing at right. If your jointer's fence doesn't have any mounting holes in it, consider drilling a couple in it for mounting auxiliary fences like the tall fence shown here. Alternatively, you can temporarily affix the auxiliary fence to the jointer fence with double-sided tape—just make sure to use the cloth-type tape to get a good bond. You'll find that you'll get an even better bond if you temporarily compress the auxiliary fence to the jointer fence with a handscrew or clamp.

Skewed fence. A skewed fence is a different type of auxiliary fence—this one is wedge-shaped to present your workpiece to the cutterhead at an angle, as shown in the drawing at right. Angling the workpiece like this produces the same effect that you get when you skew a hand plane at an angle on a workpiece to create a more shearing cut. A shearing cut tends to produce cleaner cuts in highly figured and squirrelly woods.

TALL FENCE AND SKEWED FENCE

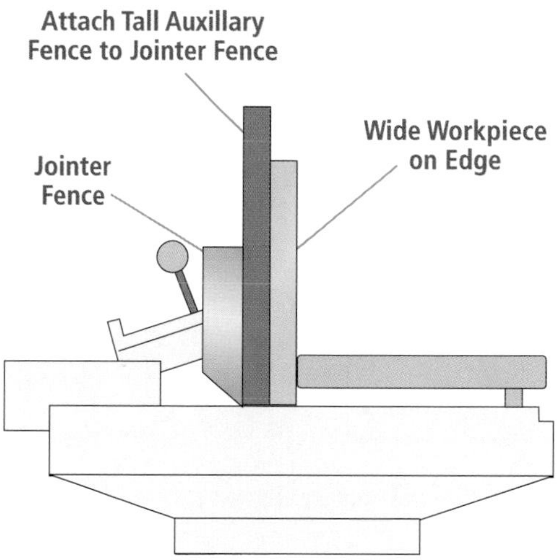

Attach Tall Auxiliary Fence to Jointer Fence

Jointer Fence

Wide Workpiece on Edge

END VIEW

Wedge-Shaped Auxiliary Fence Creates Skewed Cut

Jointer Fence

Workpiece

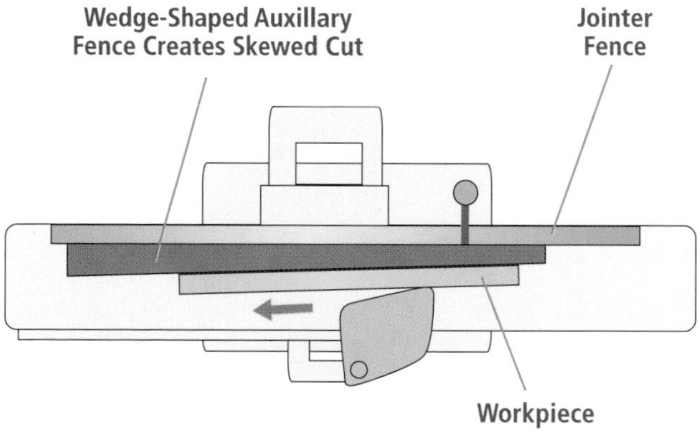

TOP VIEW

Face-Jointing

The number one rule for face-jointing is never pass your hand directly over the cutterhead. The problem with this rule is you still need to apply downward pressure to the workpiece as it passes over the cutterhead. The solution is to use some form of push block—and one in each hand works best.

The trick to face-jointing is knowing where to apply pressure—and when—with your push blocks. The drawing at right illustrates the correct technique.

DEALING WITH CUP

Dealing with a cupped board is a two-step process. The first step is to remove the cup from one face as shown in the bottom drawing. This creates a flat reference face that can be used by the planer to create a flat parallel face. It's important to realize that using this technique will generally greatly reduce the thickness of the workpiece, as shown. Don't be tempted to just stick a cupped board in a planer—all the planer will do is produce a thinner cupped board (see page 64 for more on this).

Set the jointer for a light cut (around $1/16"$) and, using push blocks, pass the board slowly over the cutterhead. Don't worry about keeping the edge of the board perfectly flush with the fence—you can joint a perpendicular edge after you've jointed the face flat. Take as many light passes as necessary until the face is flat.

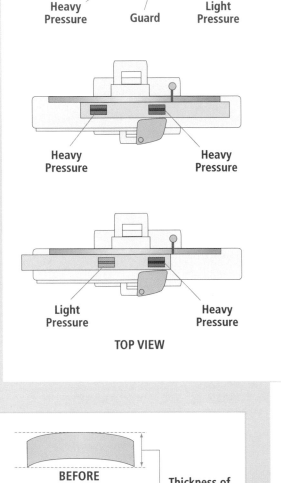

FACE-JOINTING SEQUENCE

Workpiece · Push Block · Feed Direction · Heavy Pressure · Guard · Light Pressure

Heavy Pressure · Heavy Pressure

Light Pressure · Heavy Pressure

TOP VIEW

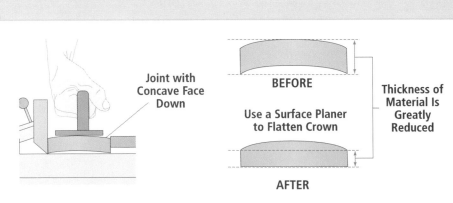

Joint with Concave Face Down

BEFORE

Use a Surface Planer to Flatten Crown

AFTER

Thickness of Material Is Greatly Reduced

Mark face with pencil

One of the simplest tricks you can use to check whether the entire face of a workpiece is flat is to lightly scribble a pencil mark across the face of the board (top photo). Stop between passes and check the face. When the pencil line is gone, the face is flat.

Keep jointed edge against fence

Whenever possible, keep the straightest edge of your workpiece firmly up against the face of your fence. Rough or crooked edges make maintaining uniform pressure difficult because the workpiece can be jostled as the rough edge rides against the fence, as illustrated in the middle drawing.

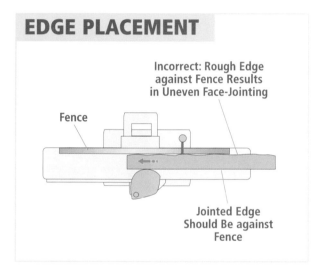

EDGE PLACEMENT

Fence

Incorrect: Rough Edge against Fence Results in Uneven Face-Jointing

Jointed Edge Should Be against Fence

Use push blocks

If you have a grout float–style push block, set it directly over the end of the workpiece and apply downward pressure as it engages the cutterhead. Since grout float–style push blocks don't have a lip, they work extremely well for applying pressure to the workpiece as it passes over the cutterhead, as shown in the bottom photo. This is important for getting an even cut and prevents the workpiece from chattering (bouncing as it comes in contact with the cutterhead) and producing a ribbed cut. The disadvantage to grout float–style push blocks is that they can slip during the cut. The method we prefer is to use a lipped push block at the rear of the workpiece to push it and a float-style push block up front to apply downward pressure.

Check with a straightedge

When you think the face is flat, turn off your jointer and check the face for flatness with a straightedge as shown in the top photo. The best way to do this is to place a straightedge on edge and hold both up to a light or a sunlit window. Any light showing under the straightedge indicates a low spot and you'll need to continue face-jointing.

Make second pass

Continue jointing the face as shown in the middle photo as needed until the face checks flat. Alternatively, once you have the majority of the face flat, you can thickness-plane (see pages 64–65). Once you've established a parallel face, flip the workpiece over and take another pass to remove any low spots—check again for flatness, and plane or joint as needed.

Check for square

Finally, check the adjacent edge of the workpiece for square with a try square as shown in the bottom photo. Odds are that it won't be square and you'll need to edge-joint. For more on this, see pages 54–57.

Jointing Short, Long, and Heavy Stock

Anyone who's ever bought a power tool and looked through the owner's manual knows that the first few pages are devoted to various types of warnings. Most of these are common sense—but sadly, many of them are ignored. Although they're all important, there's one special warning that we'd like to emphasize. And that's the minimum stock length that can be safely jointed. Small bench-top jointers typically have a minimum length around 8"; on larger jointers it's usually around 10" to 12". Don't try to joint pieces shorter than this! More jointer accidents occur because of trying to joint short pieces than for any other reason. Read and heed the manufacturer's recommendations.

The challenge to jointing long or heavy stock is that the weight of the workpiece tends to tilt it as you joint a face or an edge. The solution to this is to use some form of support.

Infeed/outfeed support

Trying to joint long or heavy stock on a short bed jointer without using some form of support is an accident waiting to happen. The weight of an unsupported workpiece can tilt the piece up, exposing the cutterhead at either the beginning or the end of the cut. To prevent this, position one (or better yet, two) supports on each end of the jointer to fully prop up the workpiece through the entire cut, as shown in the top photo. You can purchase infeed/outfeed support (page 47) or build your own (see pages 116–121).

Featherboards

Another way to help support a long or heavy workpiece is to use a featherboard to press it into the fence and/or table. Featherboards can be magnetic (middle photo) or clamp in place (bottom photo). In either case, they can help control the cut—particularly with really long or heavy stock.

Planer Setup

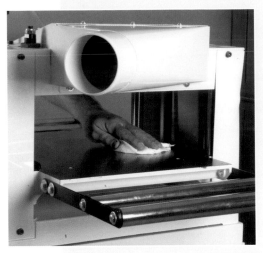

As with using a jointer (pages 52–53), it's a good idea to do a "pre-flight" check on your planer—especially if you're going to plane a lot of wood. The key elements to check are the bed, the infeed and outfeed tables, depth of cut, infeed-outfeed support, and dust collection.

Clean the bed

On most planers, a workpiece is pressed down into the planer bed by the feed rollers to advance the stock through the planer. If the bed of the planer isn't clean and maintained properly (top photo), friction can occur, resulting in a rough cut. Make sure the planer bed is free from chips and dust and coated with the proper lubricant (see page 157).

Check the infeed/outfeed tables

The first thing to do when getting ready to plane wood—especially if it's a large job—is to double-check the support tables or rollers to make sure that they're aligned with the bed of the planer. To do this, place an accurate straightedge on edge on the bed of the planer so that it extends out onto the support table or rollers, as shown in the middle photo. Then adjust the table or rollers up or down until they're flush with the bottom edge of the straightedge. This is one of the simplest ways to help prevent snipe (for more on this, see pages 66–68).

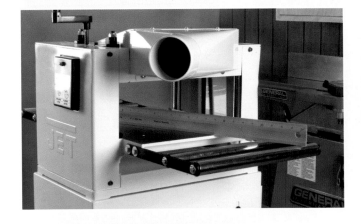

Adjust the depth of cut

Once the planer's support tables or rollers are aligned, the next step is to adjust the depth of cut. If you're planing rough-sawn wood, insert a scrap piece into the planer and then lower the head (or raise the table) until the cutterhead contacts the scrap. This gives you an idea of where to start. Then back off the cut a quarter turn to release the scrap and adjust for the depth of cut desired. Here again, consult the owner's manual for maximum cut. Just remember that lighter cuts will produce a smoother surface and will be easier on the planer.

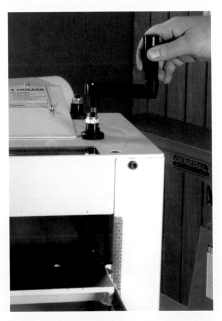

Add infeed/outfeed support

Unless you're planing fairly short stock (make sure it's longer than the recommended minimum width), it's always a good idea to add some form of support to either the infeed, the outfeed, or both, as shown in the middle photo below. Position a support as needed and adjust its height so that it's just a hair lower than the planer's support tables or rollers. If you adjust it to the same height, the front edge of the workpiece can often dip a bit and ram into the side of the support instead of passing over it.

Hook up dust collection

Planing wood creates a horrendous amount of dust and chips. All planers should be hooked up to some form of dust control, as shown in the bottom photo, even if it's as simple as a shop vacuum. You need to protect your lungs from this EPA-defined carcinogen. At the same time, you'll keep your shop from being coated with a layer of dust and chips.

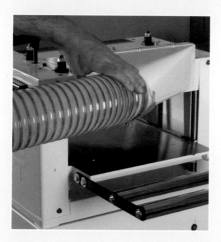

PLANER SAFETY LIST

1. Always wear eye protection.

2. Do not wear loose clothing, long sleeves, or jewelry when operating a planer.

3. Guards should be in place and used at all times.

4. Never exceed the maximum depth of cut.

5. Always keep hands and fingers away from the cutterhead.

6. Make all adjustments and repairs with the power turned off.

7. Keep the work area clean.

8. Never leave a planer running unattended; always turn it off before stepping away from it.

9. Planer blades are extremely sharp; use caution when cleaning or changing them.

10. Whenever possible, use some form of chip and dust collection.

11. Use suitable support for long or heavy workpieces.

12. Never perform any planing operation with the cutterhead or drive guard removed.

13. Do not plane material shorter than the manufacturer's recommended minimum length.

14. Check the feed rollers occasionally to make sure that there are no chips or sawdust between any components.

15. Plane only sound lumber—there should be no loose knots and as few tight knots as possible.

16. Make sure the workpiece is free from nails, screws, stones, and other foreign matter before planing.

17. Never stand directly in line with either the infeed or outfeed tables.

18. Always allow the cutterhead to reach full speed before planing.

19. Keep the planer bed and infeed/outfeed tables or rollers lubricated.

20. Maintain the proper relationship between the infeed and outfeed surfaces and the cutterhead knife path.

Thickness-Planing

Surfacing wood or thickness-planing on a properly adjusted and finely tuned planer is simply a matter of feeding in the stock in one end and lifting it out the other. In a perfect world, snipe (see pages 66–68) does not exist. In the real world, it's a fact of life. There are a few simple rules to remember when thickness-planing, with grain direction, feed rate, and depth of cut being paramount.

Grain direction

As with jointing wood, grain direction is important when planing—if you want a smooth surface. For a clean and smooth cut, the grain on your workpiece should slant down toward the bed, as illustrated in the drawing at right. This way the knives can't get under the wood fibers and tear them out.

How not to deal with cup

One of the most common mistakes we've seen woodworkers make when using a planer is to try to flatten cupped or warped stock with just the planer alone. Granted, you will get a thicknessed board with parallel faces—the problem is, the cup or warp will still be there. The reason for this is that the infeed and outfeed rollers of the planer are strong enough to press the board flat as it passes under the cutterhead, as shown in the bottom drawing. But as soon as the board is free from this pressure, it'll spring back to its original form—it'll just be thinner.

Try a skewed cut

If you're planing highly figured wood or wood with squirrelly grain, it may help to feed the workpiece into the planer at a slight angle, as shown in the bottom photo. Skewing the workpiece produces more of a shearing cut, which tends to result in smoother surfaces in difficult woods.

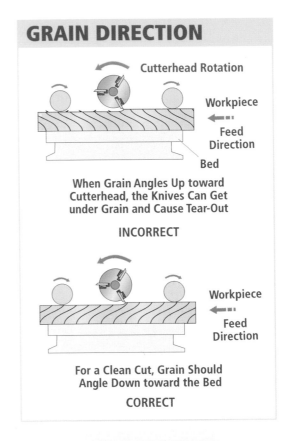

GRAIN DIRECTION

Cutterhead Rotation

Workpiece

Feed Direction

Bed

When Grain Angles Up toward Cutterhead, the Knives Can Get under Grain and Cause Tear-Out

INCORRECT

Workpiece

Feed Direction

For a Clean Cut, Grain Should Angle Down toward the Bed

CORRECT

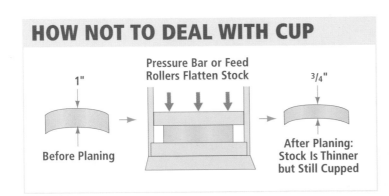

HOW NOT TO DEAL WITH CUP

1"

Pressure Bar or Feed Rollers Flatten Stock

3/4"

Before Planing

After Planing: Stock Is Thinner but Still Cupped

Feed the stock into the planer

Once you've set up your planer and have adjusted it for the desired cut (see page 62), you're ready to plane. Place one end of the workpiece on the planer bed and lower the opposite end until it's almost level, and feed it slowly into the planer until the infeed roller takes over (middle photo). A slight lift to the board will help prevent snipe as it contacts the cutterhead. In no case should the end of the board slant down, or snipe will occur. If the feed rollers on your planer are adjusted properly, you shouldn't have to push the workpiece into the planer—the rollers will move it through at the correct speed. If the planer bogs down and the workpiece pauses, odds are that you're taking too deep of a cut. Don't push. Instead, adjust for a lighter cut.

Grab and lift

Just as with pushing, you shouldn't have to pull a board through a planer. Admittedly, this is required sometimes, particularly with wide stock on a planer with rubber rollers. The rollers just can't grip the board sufficiently to push it past the cutterhead. Keeping rollers clean will help, but taking light cuts is the best way to avoid a tug-of-war. Since snipe occurs at the end of a planer's cut, one way to reduce it is to gently lift the end of the board up as it nears the end of the cut, as shown in the bottom photo (see pages 66–68 for more on this).

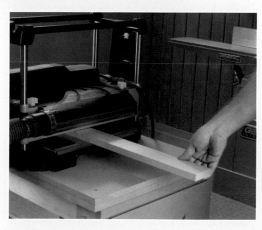

REMOVE LIKE AMOUNTS FROM EACH FACE

Even when kiln-dried, lumber is still wetter at the core of the stock than on the outer surfaces. If you were to remove material from just a single face, you'd expose the wet core on one side, and the workpiece would warp. To prevent this, it's important to always remove like amounts of material from alternating faces of the stock, as illustrated in the drawing below.

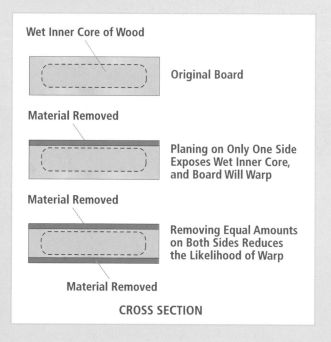

Wet Inner Core of Wood

Original Board

Material Removed

Planing on Only One Side Exposes Wet Inner Core, and Board Will Warp

Material Removed

Removing Equal Amounts on Both Sides Reduces the Likelihood of Warp

Material Removed

CROSS SECTION

Dealing with Snipe

Snipe—where a thickness planer cuts or dishes the ends of a board thinner than the middle portion of a board—is so common that many woodworkers resign themselves to always having it. That's too bad because there are techniques you can use to minimize snipe. Sure, if your planer in not adjusted properly and the workpiece isn't supported, snipe will occur no matter what you do in terms of technique. But if you follow the planing procedures described here, you can reduce this annoying problem.

Why snipe occurs

There are a number of causes of snipe. Some are operator-related, but many can be caused by the planer. For instance, if your knives are dull, they tend to lift the end of the board as it enters the planer. The pressure rollers and table rollers often take much of the blame—and rightfully so. As a board enters or exits a planer, it's only in contact with one of the rollers. And the pressure of the roller often cocks the board up slightly into the cutterhead, resulting in a deeper cut, as illustrated in the drawing at right. Basically, the table rollers and/or the pressure rollers do not uniformly support the workpiece as it passes through the planer.

WHY SNIPE OCCURS

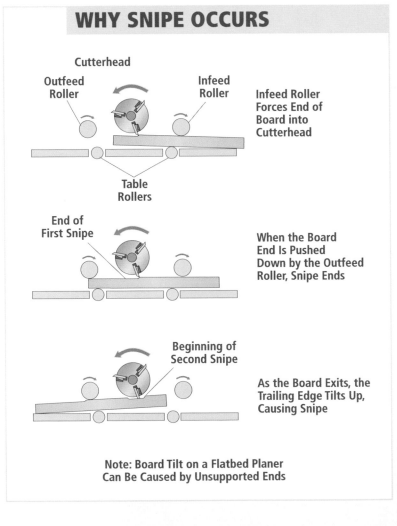

Cutterhead
Outfeed Roller
Infeed Roller
Table Rollers

Infeed Roller Forces End of Board into Cutterhead

End of First Snipe

When the Board End Is Pushed Down by the Outfeed Roller, Snipe Ends

Beginning of Second Snipe

As the Board Exits, the Trailing Edge Tilts Up, Causing Snipe

Note: Board Tilt on a Flatbed Planer Can Be Caused by Unsupported Ends

SNIPE ANATOMY

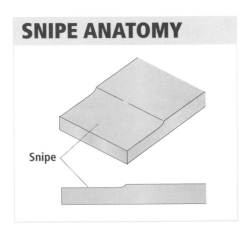

Snipe

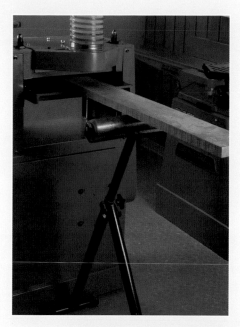

Infeed/outfeed support

One of the best ways to combat snipe is to fully support the ends of the workpiece as it enters and leaves the planer, as shown in the top photo. Alternatively, you can raise the outside ends of your extension tables a few thousandths of an inch above the planer bed. This helps prevent the workpiece from cocking up into the cutterhead.

Lift up at end of cut

Probably the most commonly used technique to fight snipe is to lift the end of a board up as it exits the planer, as shown in the middle photo. In effect what you're doing here is applying some leverage to the board (via the outfeed roller) to offset the natural tendency of the board to lift up once its end is free from the downward pressure applied by the infeed roller. The key here is gentle pressure: If you lift up hard and often, you'll end up weakening the springs on the outfeed roller.

Insert boards end-to-end

Here's a slick way to avoid snipe when you're planning multiple pieces that are the same thickness. **Safety note:** You should use this technique only when all the pieces are the *identical* thickness—if some are thinner, they won't be captured by the rollers and could kick back when they come in contact with the cutterhead. The way this works is simple. By feeding the stock into the planer so that pieces butt end-to-end (as shown in the bottom photo), you'll have the infeed and outfeed rollers constantly under tension—just as if you were planing a long board. Since snipe only occurs at the start or finish of a cut, it can only occur on the first and last pieces fed into the planer this way.

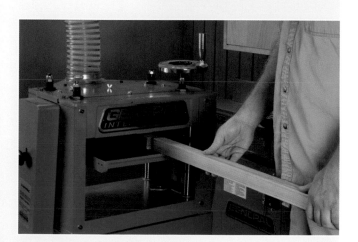

Use an auxiliary table

You can totally eliminate snipe caused by table rollers by using a flat auxiliary table, as shown in the top photo. Alternatively, you can remove the rollers and install an auxiliary table with cleats on the bottom to fit in the spaces left by the rollers. If you cover the table top with plastic laminate or melamine, you'll help reduce friction.

Cut off, sand, or scrape the ends

Sadly, it's almost impossible to totally eliminate snipe, so you'll end up having to deal with some. There are three common ways to do this. Some woodworkers cut their stock long to begin with and simply cut the snipe off the ends once the board is planed (middle photo). Wasteful, yes—but effective. If the snipe is minimal, you can sand out the variation—you'll find that a random-orbit sander does a great job of this. For deeper snipe, start by first smoothing the transition with a hand scraper before turning to sandpaper.

ANTI-SNIPE PLANERS

Manufacturers of planers are all too well aware of the problem of snipe, and most have tried various fixes over the years. Some have even been marketed as "anti-snipe" planers, but there really is no such thing. There are some improvements, though, that can help. One of these is a cutterhead lock. A cutterhead lock addresses the problem common on many smaller planers—especially those with two posts supporting the cutterhead instead of four. When you raise and lower the cutterhead, there's always some slack in the screw threads that the cutterhead rides up and down on. Without a lock, the cutterhead can pivot slightly as it comes in contact with the workpiece. A cutterhead lock feature prevents this—it allows you to manually freeze the cutterhead in position for planing.

ADD SUPPORT UNDER WARP

Cup Method # 1

Flatten One Face with
a Hand Plane or Jointer
before Thickness-Planing

Cup Method # 2

Support Wide Board
with Narrower Scrap

Cleat to Keep
Workpiece
from Shifting
While Planing

Sled

Insert Shims
to Support
Warped Ends

Removing Warp

As we've mentioned previously, running a warped board though a planer will only result in a thinner warped board (see page 64). There are, however, a couple of techniques you can use to remove warp with a planer and some type of support; see below. The best way, though, is to use a jointer in conjunction with a planer, as described below.

Add support under warp

For a cupped board, try slipping a narrower scrap board under the warped board as shown in the top drawing. This will allow the planer to create a flat foundation surface without flexing the board. For boards that are warped along their length, build a sled and add shims under the warped areas as shown. This, too, will let the planer create a flat foundation surface. Just make sure to secure the shims to the sled and the board to the shims with double-sided tape.

Flatten one face

The most reliable way to remove cup is to place the board on the jointer with the concave face down, as shown in the middle photo. Set the jointer for a light cut and, using push blocks, pass the board slowly over the cutterhead. Don't worry about keeping the edge of the board perfectly flush with the fence—you can joint a perpendicular edge after you've jointed the face flat. Take as many light passes as necessary until the face is flat.

Thickness-plane the opposite face

Once you've got one face jointed flat, you can create a second parallel face with the planer, as shown in the bottom photo. Take light cuts and continue planing until the desired thickness is achieved.

Squaring Up Stock

None of the wood you buy will be perfectly square or flat. Just because a board is surfaced on all four sides doesn't mean it's square. Most likely it will be thicknessed accurately, but it won't be flat or square. The only way to ensure that it's both is for you to make it so. The squaring-up sequence described here is one of the keys to successful woodworking. If you don't start with square stock, virtually nothing else you do with the stock will work out right: Joinery won't fit, you'll experience gaps in your glue joints, and your projects won't hold up well over time.

Face-joint

The first step to squaring up stock is to joint one face smooth, as shown in the bottom photo. Use push blocks to press the workpiece firmly against the infeed and outfeed tables as you make the cut. Remember to never pass your hands directly over the cutterhead, and to shift your weight to the outfeed table once the stock has passed the cutterhead. Don't worry about keeping the edge perfectly flush with the fence—you'll take care of this in the next step.

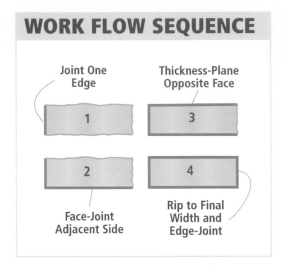

WORK FLOW SEQUENCE

Joint One Edge — 1

Face-Joint Adjacent Side — 2

Thickness-Plane Opposite Face — 3

Rip to Final Width and Edge-Joint — 4

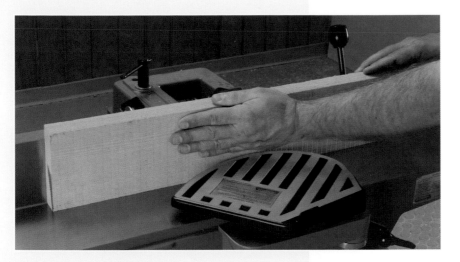

Edge-joint

After one face is jointed flat, the next step to squaring stock is to joint an edge perpendicular to the flattened face. Press the jointed face up firmly against the fence and take a series of light cuts until the entire edge is jointed flat, as shown in the top photo. Here again, you'll want to shift your weight to the out-feed table once the stock passes over the cutterhead.

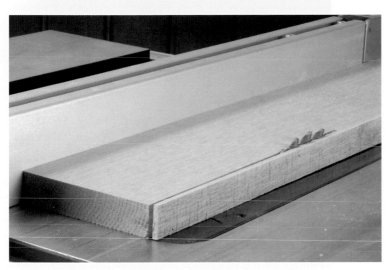

Rip to rough width

Now that you've got two square edges, you can go ahead and rip your stock to width, as shown in the middle photo. We always rip the board just a hair wide and then clean up this edge in the next step. Alternatively, you can move ahead to thickness-planing, and rip your boards to width after they've been thicknessed.

MARKING CUTS

When you're prepping stock for a project—particularly when the project calls for a lot of parts—it's easy to lose track of which edges on your parts have been machined. That's why we always mark our cuts on each workpiece as we go, as shown in the bottom photo. Something as simple as a penciled "X" or a slash is all it takes to indicate a freshly machined surface.

Clean up ripped edge

If you've ripped you parts to rough width, the next step is to clean up the ripped edge by taking a light pass on the jointer, as shown in the top photo. If you've got a lot of similarly sized parts—like rails or stiles for a set of frames—consider thickness-planing them on edge to create uniformly wide parts (see page 93 for more on this).

Thickness-plane

As soon as you create two flat perpendicular edges, you can create two parallel flat faces. The best tool for the job here is the planer. Place the flattened face against the bed of the planer, adjust for a light cut, and feed the board into the planer as shown in the middle photo. Let the infeed roller take over and push the board past the cutterhead. When it comes out the other side, lift the end of the board lightly to help prevent snipe.

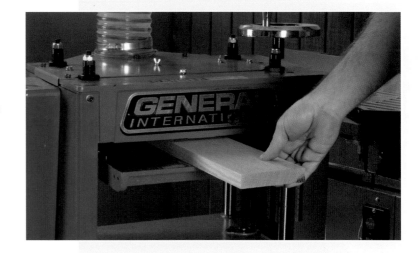

Trim workpiece to length

All that's left is to trim your parts to length. Start by first cutting one end square, then measure the desired length, and mark and cut the part to length as shown in the bottom photo.

Using a Portable Power Planer

A power planer is neither a planer nor a jointer; it's really a motorized hand plane. And it's a terrific tool for removing a precise shaving from a project. Trim carpenters love portable planers because they can remove a lot of material in a short time.

Clamp workpiece securely

The number one rule for using a power planer is to always secure your workpiece to a stable foundation, as shown in the middle photo. The last thing you want is to turn your power planer into a workpiece ejector. Err on the side of more clamps, rather than too few clamps.

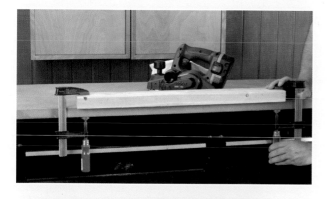

Adjust the depth of cut

The next thing to do with a power planer is to adjust it to the desired depth of cut. As always, we recommend taking a series of lighter cuts, instead of one heavy cut. The cut of most power planers is adjusted by turning a large knob on the front of the planer to the depth indicated on the scale, as shown in the bottom photo. Note that virtually every power planer has a "zero" or "P" (for "Park") position that sets the blades up into the planer so they don't protrude at all. The blades should be in this position whenever the planer is not in use.

PORTABLE POWER PLANER SAFETY RULES

1. Always secure the material being planed. Never hold it in your hand or across legs. Unstable support can cause the blades to bind, causing loss of control and injury.

2. Always start the planer and allow it to come up to full speed before contacting the workpiece with the blade.

3. Check your workpiece for nails or other fasteners that could damage the blades.

4. Disconnect the battery or unplug the planer before making adjustments, adding accessories, or making repairs.

5. After changing blades, make sure to rotate the blade cylinder by hand to make sure the blades are not hitting any portion of the blade-head housing.

6. Always hold the planer firmly with both hands for maximum control.

7. Never pull the planer backward over the workpiece.

8. Do not put fingers or other objects into the chip ejector or clean out chips while the tool is running.

9. Never place the planer down until the blade is completely at rest.

10. Portable planer blades are extremely sharp; use caution when cleaning or changing them.

Basic planing technique

With the workpiece clamped securely, stand comfortably and hold the planer with both hands. Place the front shoe on the workpiece so blades are not in contact with the workpiece, and start the planer. With pressure on the front shoe, feed the planer steadily forward until the rear shoe fully engages the workpiece, as shown in the top photo. Then gradually transfer pressure to the rear shoe and continue planing to the end of the cut. Use progressive cuts until you've removed the desired amount of material.

Add support if necessary

Whenever you plane a narrow strip of wood, it's a good idea to provide additional support to the workpiece to prevent the planer from tipping sideways during the cut. The simplest way to do this is to clamp a wide scrap of wood (like the 2×4 shown in the middle photo) to the side of the workpiece. This creates a stable platform for the planer, and you'll get a smoother, more accurate cut.

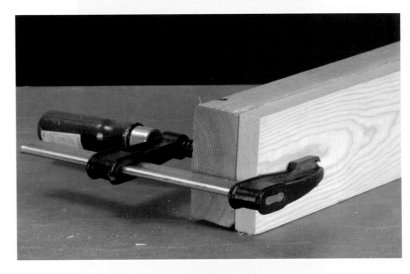

Cutting bevels

Bevels are easy to create with a power planer, as shown in the bottom photo. The only problem here is that since you don't have an adjustable-angle fence, you need to carefully lay out the angle on both ends of the workpiece and stop frequently to see how you're doing. Note that even with careful layout, it's tough to cut an accurate bevel. With a little ingenuity, you could fasten an angled fence to the planer to guide it for a more precise cut.

Cutting chamfers

Another thing a power planer excels at is cutting quick chamfers. Most power planers have a groove running the length of their base designed especially for this. This V-groove will ride along the edge of the workpiece and will press up against adjacent sides to create a very nice chamfer, as shown in the top photo. This is one situation where you can safely take a deeper cut, as you're removing much less wood. As always, it's a good idea to make a test cut on a scrap piece first.

Using a fence

Most quality power planers come with a fence that can be used with the planer to make accurate cuts and rabbets. An auxiliary fence (like the one shown in the middle photo) is also a good way to add extra support to the planer for almost any cut. Just slide the fence into the desired position and tighten the lock knob. Then butt the fence up against the side of the workpiece and make the cut.

Cutting rabbets

One of the features we like best about a portable power planer is that it makes it extremely easy to cut accurate rabbets. Here's where a solid auxiliary fence comes in handy. Adjust the fence to match the desired width of the rabbet, and take a test cut on a scrap piece to make sure it's the correct width. Then adjust the planer for a light cut and make a series of passes until the desired depth of the rabbet is reached.

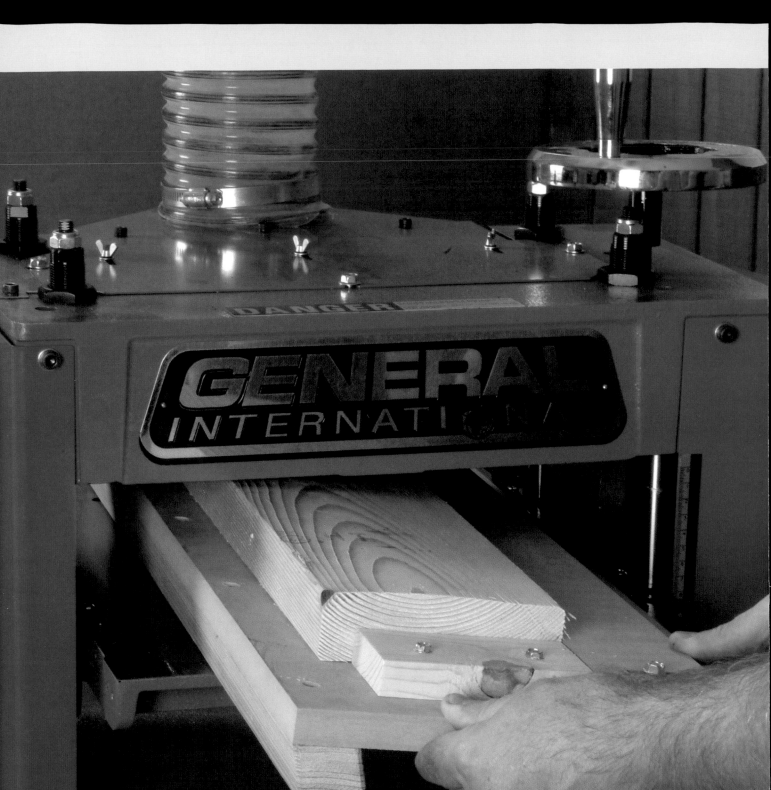

4 Advanced Jointer and Planer Techniques

Most woodworkers think of the jointer and planer as single-purpose machines; that is, one joints edges, and the other thickness-planes. But with knowledge and some simple jigs, you can do a lot more with both machines. As a matter of fact, some of the techniques described in this chapter work better than the "standard" methods used, especially those that are done on a table saw, which has a tendency to leave saw marks on a workpiece. In this chapter, we'll show you how to cut bevels, chamfers, and rabbets on the jointer, how to taper a post, how to make raised panels, and how to joint plywood and end grain. Planer tricks include ganged cuts, planing on edge, planing thin and short stock, making molding, and cutting long and wide tapers on the planer.

In addition to flattening, squaring, and thicknessing stock, jointers and planers can be pressed into service to handle a wide variety of specialty jobs like cutting long, smooth tapers, as shown here.

Beveling on a Jointer

A jointer excels at cutting smooth, accurate bevels. All it takes is a properly adjusted fence and a firm grip. In order to cut a bevel on a jointer, you'll need to first lay out the intended angle on the work-piece with a sliding bevel or with a protractor.

Tilt the fence

To adjust the jointer's fence, loosen the fence clamp to friction-tight and then tilt the fence to the desired angle, as shown in the top right photo and the illustration at right. To get an exact angle, place an adjustable-angle gauge or sliding bevel set to the desired angle on the jointer bed. Position the handle on the bed and the blade on the fence, and tilt the fence until there's no gap between it and the blade. Then press the workpiece firmly against the fence to make the cut.

Add a support strip

Whenever you tilt the fence on a jointer, the inclined plane of the fence and gravity tend to work against you—the workpiece tends to slide down, resulting in a wavy bevel. Here's a simple trick to avoid this. Just clamp a strip of wood next to the fence so its distance from the fence matches the width of the bevel, as shown in the bottom photo. This creates a stop, which prevents the workpiece from sliding down. You can also attach the strip to the jointer's fence or bed with double-sided tape as shown here.

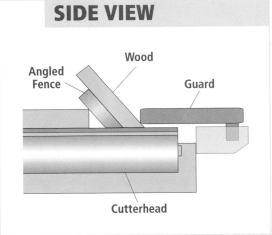

SIDE VIEW

Angled Fence

Wood

Guard

Cutterhead

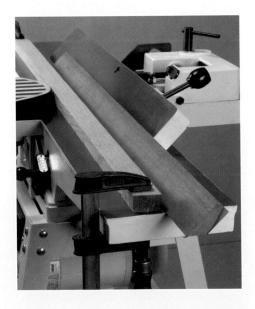

ALTERNATIVE METHOD SIDE VIEW

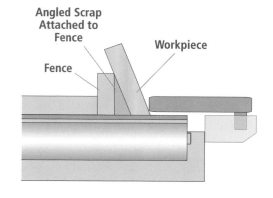

Angled Scrap Attached to Fence

Workpiece

Fence

Attach an auxiliary wedge to the fence

An alternative method for beveling on the jointer is to cut a wedge at the desired angle and attach it to your fence with double-sided tape, as illustrated in the drawing at left. For jointers that do not have a titling fence, this is the only way to safely bevel a workpiece. It's important that the wedge be cut thick enough so that it will fully support the workpiece but also extend it out far enough so that the top of the fence doesn't interfere with the cut, as shown in the middle photo.

Joint the bevel

To use the auxiliary wedge, just butt the face of your workpiece firmly against the wedge and guide the workpiece over the cutterhead, taking care to keep the workpiece in constant contact, as shown in the bottom photo. Here again, an additional support strip (as described on page 78) will help ensure an accurate cut.

Chamfering on a Jointer

The big advantage that a jointer offers over other tools for chamfering is that it creates a perfectly smooth cut. There are two basic methods to cutting chamfers on the jointer. The first method is to tilt the fence to 45 degrees and press the workpiece against the fence to make the cut. The problem with this method is that it's difficult to prevent the workpiece from sliding around as you cut the chamfer. A more accurate method (shown on the opposite page) uses beveled strips attached to the jointer's infeed and outfeed tables to guide the workpiece.

Tilt the fence

Start by tilting your fence to 45 degrees, as shown in the top right photo. Most jointers have a built-in stop for this. Even so, it's a good idea to check this angle with the angled head of a combination square to make sure the stop is adjusted properly.

Attach a guide strip to the table

To prevent the workpiece from shifting on the tilted fence, attach a guide strip to the infeed and outfeed tables of the jointer as shown in the middle photo. Its position will define the width of the chamfer.

Joint the chamfer

Adjust the jointer for the desired depth of cut, and slide the workpiece smoothly over the cutterhead as shown in the bottom photo. Take as many passes as needed to create the desired chamfer width.

ALTERNATIVE METHOD

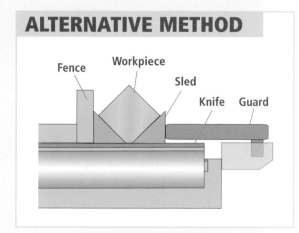

Fence   Workpiece   Sled   Knife   Guard

Attach strips to bed

To accurately cut chamfers on a jointer whose fence doens't tilt, start by cutting a pair of 45-degree strips from scrap wood. It's best that they be roughly the same length as your jointer. The easiest way to attach the strips to the jointer is with double-sided carpet tape. Attach one strip so that it butts up against the fence, and then position the remaining strip away from the first strip the desired width of the chamfer, as illustrated in the top drawing and the middle photo.

Cut the chamfer

Now that you've positioned the strips, all that's left is to cut the chamfer. Position the workpiece in the trough formed by the strips, and push it past the cutterhead as shown in the bottom photo. Rotate the piece as desired to cut chamfers on the other corners of the workpiece. This type of setup lends itself well to production runs. It's a lot quieter and faster than cutting the chamfers with a router—and you'll end up with smoother cuts.

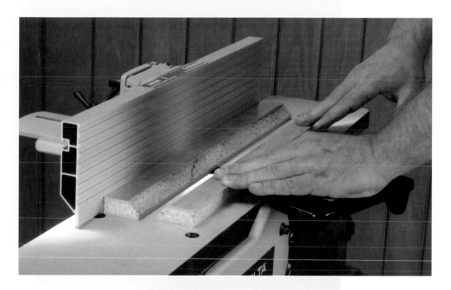

Rabbeting on a Jointer

Some jointers have a recess in the outfeed table or a special detachable rabbeting arm that allows for rabbeting, as illustrated in the middle drawing. In the case of the rabbeting arm, the jointer knives will run the full length of the bed, and access to the ends of the knives is allowed by removing the arm. The disadvantage of the recess in the outfeed table is that it limits the width of the stock that you can rabbet.

Add an auxiliary fence

If the workpiece you're rabbeting is wide, it's a good idea to attach a tall auxiliary fence to your jointer's fence, as shown in the bottom photo. If your jointer's fence doesn't have any mounting holes in it, consider drilling a couple in it for mounting auxiliary fences like the tall fence shown here. Alternatively, you can temporarily affix the auxiliary fence to the jointer fence with double-sided tape—just make sure to use the cloth type to get a good bond. You'll find that you'll get an even better bond if you temporarily compress the auxiliary fence to the jointer fence with a hand screw or clamp.

RABBETING LEDGE

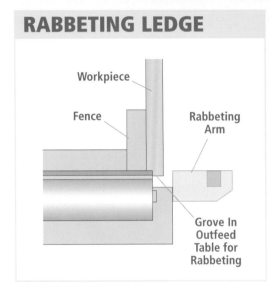

Workpiece

Fence

Rabbeting Arm

Grove In Outfeed Table for Rabbeting

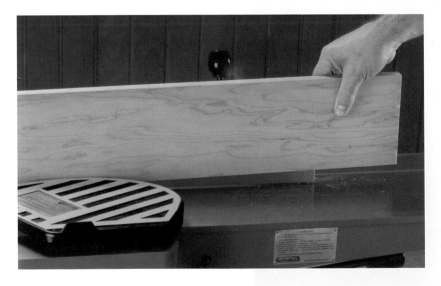

Adjust the fence

Next, slide the fence over to set the rabbet width, as shown in the top photo. Note that on jointers where the fence doesn't slide over far enough, you'll need to shim out the auxiliary fence with scraps.

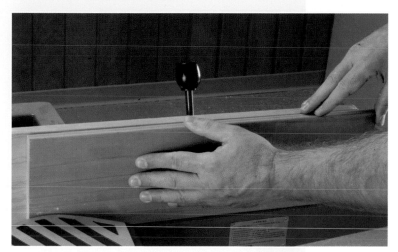

Start the cut

To joint a rabbet, start by setting the infeed table depth—odds are that you'll need to make multiple passes to achieve the desired depth, as shown in the middle photo. Make a trial cut on a scrap piece, and adjust the fence as necessary to get the desired width. **Safety note:** If you had to remove the guard, turn off the jointer between passes and when adjusting the infeed table, as the jointer knives are exposed.

Finish the cut

Take light cuts and check the depth of the rabbet often. Continue jointing until the desired rabbet depth is achieved, as shown in the bottom photo.

Tapering a Post

Clean, smooth tapers are easy to make on the jointer by following the simple procedure described here. The advantage that a jointer has over other tapering methods—especially the table saw—is that the completed leg or post requires virtually no sanding. There are no saw marks to remove—the faces of the leg are smooth, and the corners are crisp.

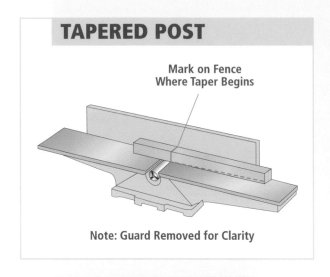

TAPERED POST

Mark on Fence Where Taper Begins

Note: Guard Removed for Clarity

Mark start of taper

To taper a post or leg, begin by marking a reference line on all four sides of each piece, as shown in the middle photo. Measure down from the top to the desired starting point of the taper, and then use a try square to transfer this mark around to all four sides. You'll use these marks to position the post or leg on the jointer to make the cut.

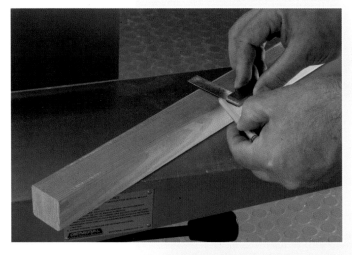

Mark the fence

The next step is to mark a reference line on the fence of the jointer to identify the front edge of the outfeed table. Instead of marking directly on the fence, we often add a strip of masking tape to the fence and then mark it with a pen, as shown in the bottom photo. Now when you align the mark on the post with the mark on the fence, you'll know where the cut starts. Note: Instead of marking the top dead-center point of the cutterhead, marking the edge of the table allows for a final cleanup pass to remove the dished cut that the knives make.

Position the post

The basic idea here is to align the marks that you made on the post with those on the fence, and then slowly and carefully lower the post onto the cutterhead to start the cut, as shown in the top photo. Although this may sound scary, it's really quite easy after you've practiced a bit. Note: Since most tapered posts or legs will be joined to other parts, it's best to complete all joinery on the square post before tapering it.

Lower and cut

Once you've got the marks aligned, gently move the guard out of the way and slowly lower the post onto the cutterhead. As soon as it makes contact, start pushing the post forward as shown in the middle photo. If you hesitate here, you'll likely get a burn mark—especially if you're working with cherry. We suggest you try this a couple of times with the power off to get the feel of sliding the guard out of the way as you lower the post. Also, make sure to use a push block as shown here to protect your fingers.

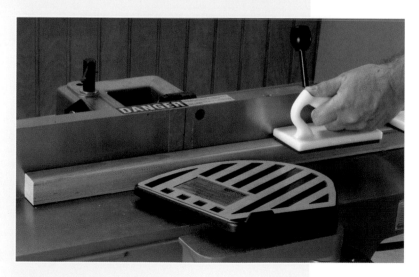

Rotate and cut

After you've made a complete pass on one side of the post, lift it up and rotate it one quarter turn. Then align the reference marks, lower the post, and make the next cut, as shown in the bottom photo. Continue until you've done all four sides (or how-ever many sides you're tapering). Stop and check the taper. Continue to take passes until you're very close to the desired taper. Then adjust the jointer for a very light pass and make a full-length pass without lowering the piece—this should remove any "dish" left by the knives.

Alternative tapering method

An alternative method of tapering on the jointer is particularly well suited for short tapers. It uses a small block of wood to set the taper angle as described below and illustrated in the top drawing.

CUT A FLAT. To use the block method of tapering, start by laying out the taper on your workpiece. **Safety note:** The taper must be longer than your jointer's throat opening for the cutterhead—otherwise it could drop into the opening. Next, remove the majority of the waste on the band saw as shown in the middle photo. Alternatively, you can nibble this portion away on the jointer by taking a series of light cuts. But it's a lot faster to remove the bulk of the waste on the band saw.

ATTACH THE BLOCK. Clamp a straightedge to the workpiece directly above the tapered line that you marked earlier. Now slide a block down the workpiece until it gets pinched between the workpiece and the ruler. Mark this position on the workpiece, remove the straightedge, and attach the block to the workpiece on the untapered side of the mark with double-sided tape, as shown in the bottom photo.

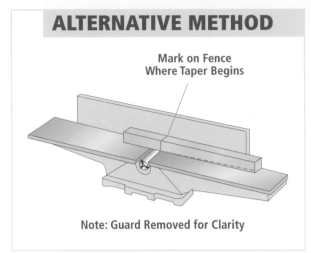

ALTERNATIVE METHOD

Mark on Fence Where Taper Begins

Note: Guard Removed for Clarity

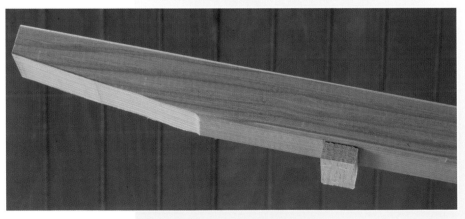

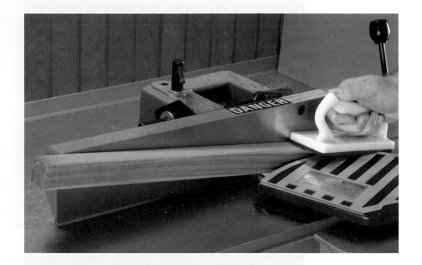

FINAL PASSES. With the majority of the waste removed and the block installed, you can take the final passes using a push block to hold the workpiece at the desired angle, as shown in the top photo. To do this, turn off the jointer, open the guard, and position the workpiece so it holds the guard open. Release the guard so that it pivots over against the workpiece, and turn on the power. Use a push block to then push the workpiece past the cutterhead. Repeat this for subsequent cuts until you reach the taper line you marked earlier..

ROTATE AND MOVE BLOCK. To taper a second side, simply reposition the block on the second side and repeat the tapering procedure as shown in the middle photo.

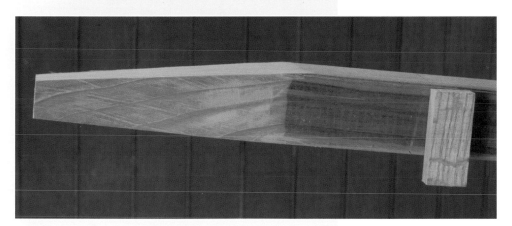

UNIFORM TAPERS

Getting tapers to match up identically can be a real challenge. One of the simplest ways to get them to match is to joint them at the same time. To do this, just temporarily attach the parts to one another with double-sided tape. Then pass this assembly over the cutterhead, as shown in the bottom photo.

Raised Panels on a Jointer

If you've ever cut tapers on the table saw and then spent hours removing the saw marks, you'll really appreciate this technique. It's surprisingly simple and requires only a shop-made angled sled.

It's possible to make raised panels on a jointer, as long as it has rabbeting capabilities (see pages 82–83). The method described here cuts surprisingly smooth panels, as long as your knives are sharp and you take light passes. The secret to making this work is a simple shop-made sled, as illustrated in the middle drawing. The sled holds the panel up at the desired angle to guide it past the cutterhead.

Remove the guard

Since you'll be passing the workpiece over the side of the jointer's infeed and outfeed tables, you'll need to remove the guard as shown in the bottom photo. **Safety note:** This exposes the knives, and extra care should be taken when using the jointer—particularly at the start and finish of the cut.

RAISED-PANEL SLED

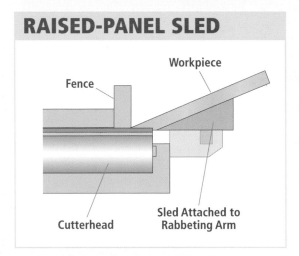

Fence

Workpiece

Cutterhead

Sled Attached to Rabbeting Arm

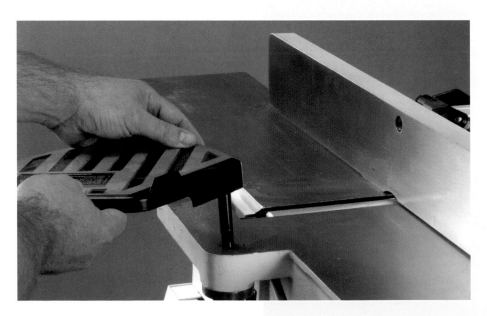

Attach the sled to jointer or stand

The sled that you make will depend on your jointer. Basically all you need are a pair of angled supports that hold a table at the desired angle. Depending on your jointer, you may or may not need to cut a notch near the knives for the sled to butt firmly up against the side of the jointer. Adding a cleat to the base of the supports will allow you to clamp the sled to the jointer as shown here.

Adjust the fence

Next, slide the jointer fence over to set the width of the field, as shown in the middle photo. Note: On jointers where the fence doesn't slide across the full width of the table, you may need to attach an auxiliary fence to the jointer's fence to set the width of the raised panel's field.

Joint the end grain first

Once you've got the sled in place, adjust the infeed table for a light cut as shown in the bottom left photo. Start cutting the raised fields on the end grain first. Any chip-out that occurs here will be removed when you joint the fields with the grain.

Rotate to long grain

Continue making passes until the jointer stops cutting—since the shoulder will ride on the infeed table when the proper depth is reached, the knives will stop cutting automatically (bottom right photo).

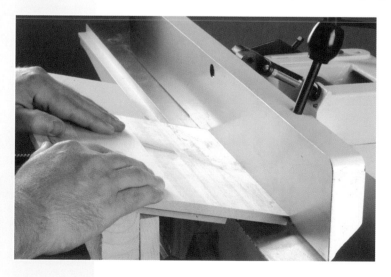

Jointing Plywood

Jointing plywood is another one of those procedures that make most woodworkers shudder. But here again, it's quite easy to do, as long as you take light cuts and your knives are sharp. Why would you want to joint the edge of plywood? We've often done it on the edges of plywood shelves where we were planning to glue on a strip to conceal the multi-layered edge. The cleaner the edge, the better the glue joint (see the photos at right). One thing to keep in mind: Plywood does contain a high glue content that can act as an abrasive to dull knives, so use this technique sparingly.

Preventing tear-out

The only real challenge to jointing plywood successfully is taking care to prevent tear-out at the end of the cut. The simplest way to prevent this is to clamp a scrap of wood onto the end of the plywood, as shown in the bottom photo. The scrap supports the fragile wood fibers at the end of the plywood, and any tear-out or chip-out that will arise occurs on the scrap.

Standard plywood edge. The standard factory plywood edge is rough, is often not straight, and is frequently not square.

Jointed plywood edge. By jointing the edge of plywood, you create a smooth, square, straight edge that will butt cleanly up against other surfaces.

Jointing End Grain

Even though most woodworkers would never consider jointing end grain, it's quite doable, as long as your knives are sharp and you take a light cut. Here again, a cleaner edge creates a better surface for gluing or joinery. Notice the difference between saw-cut end grain (left middle photo) and jointed end grain (right middle photo). The only concern when jointing end grain is chip-out as you complete the cut. There are two methods to prevent this.

Make end cuts first

One way to prevent chip-out when jointing end grain is to start jointing the end grain and then stop after about 2" to 3", as illustrated in the drawing below. Then flip the workpiece end for end and finish the cut. Be careful not to go past the previously jointed end grain, or it will chip out.

Clamp on scrap

Another method is to clamp a sacrificial scrap piece to the end of the workpiece and joint as usual, as shown in the bottom photo. This way any chip-out that occurs will be on the scrap wood.

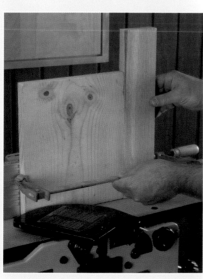

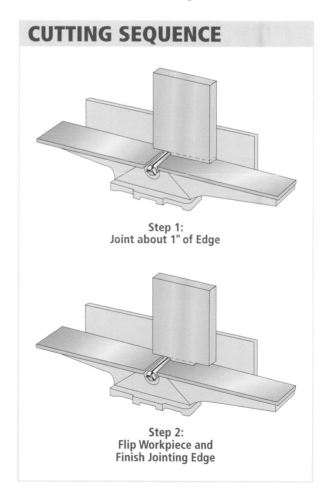

CUTTING SEQUENCE

Step 1:
Joint about 1" of Edge

Step 2:
Flip Workpiece and
Finish Jointing Edge

Ganged Planer Cuts

Planing multiple pieces at the same time—commonly referred to as a ganged cut—is a standard practice in many shops. Ganging up cuts makes work go by faster and can actually help reduce snipe; see below.

Width and thickness requirements

There is one big rule, however, for making ganged cuts: The width and thickness of the pieces that you are planing must match. For example, if you were to plane varying-width workpieces, as illustrated in the top drawing, the cutterhead could grab one of the narrower pieces and shoot it out of the planer. A similar situation could occur when thickness-planing.

Planing in bulk

There is a way you can get around the width variations when planing on edge (see page 93), and that's to temporarily secure the pieces to one another with double-sided tape (middle photo). This way the planer can't grab a narrower piece and eject it.

Stagger the pieces

If you are working with similar-sized parts, stagger them as you feed them into the planer, as shown in the bottom photo. This keeps one or more workpieces in constant contact with both of the pressure rollers (and table rollers, if applicable) and will eliminate snipe on all but the first and last pieces, as long as you continue to stagger the pieces as you feed them into the planer.

GANGED CUTS

To prevent kickback when making ganged cuts, be sure all pieces are same width or fastened to each other with double-sided carpet tape.

END VIEW

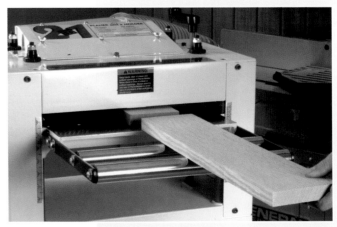

Planing on Edge

Planing on edge is a practice that's been employed in pro shops for decades. Instead of feeding the stock into the planer with the face down, stock is fed in on edge, as shown in the top photo. Planing on edge lets you create identical-width parts with smooth edges. Note that this technique works best on planers with flat beds—no rollers. Rollers can cause the workpiece to twist, resulting in a dangerous situation. The big thing to remember is, the thicker the piece the better. Most portable planers with flat beds can safely handle $3/4$"-thick stock on edge. For thinner parts, use one of the techniques described below.

Tape thin parts together

A simple way to handle thin parts that you want to plane on edge is to temporarily fasten the parts together with double-sided tape to create a wider package to present to the cutterhead.

Add auxiliary fences

Another way to handle thin parts is to add some type of support to hold the workpiece upright as it passes through the planer, as illustrated in the bottom drawing. For small runs, just tape some narrower support scraps to the side of the workpiece (middle photo). If you've got a lot of thin parts to edge-plane, consider making a sled that hooks onto the bed of your planer (see page 95). This way you can just keep feeding parts through the planer without the hassle of double-sided tape.

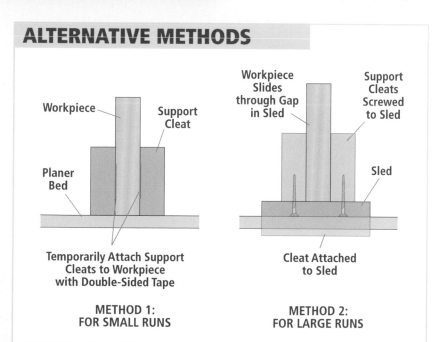

ALTERNATIVE METHODS

Workpiece — Support Cleat

Planer Bed

Temporarily Attach Support Cleats to Workpiece with Double-Sided Tape

METHOD 1:
FOR SMALL RUNS

Workpiece Slides through Gap in Sled — Support Cleats Screwed to Sled

Sled

Cleat Attached to Sled

METHOD 2:
FOR LARGE RUNS

Planing Thin or Short Stock

There always has been and there always will be debate concerning the safety of planing thin stock. Manufacturers claim that planing thin stock is hazardous, and they all list the minimum thickness that you can safely plane on their planers—often $1/4$". But woodworkers often need thinner stock—many projects call for stock less than $1/4$" thick. Although most manufacturers build in stops that limit how close the cutterhead can come to the planer's bed, woodworkers commonly get around this by using an auxiliary platform or sled that raises the workpiece closer to the cutterhead, allowing for thinner cuts.

It's important to note that planing wood this thin can cause it to break up or get shredded as it passes by the cutterhead. If you do decide to plane thin stock, make sure you don't stand directly behind or in front of the planer. Wear safety glasses, take thin cuts, and make sure your knives are sharp. There are similar concerns regarding planing short stock, but there's a simple fix for this; see the opposite page.

Tape to sled

One of the most common ways to plane thin stock is to attach it to a simple sled (a piece of plywood or MDF—medium-density fiberboard) with double-sided tape; see the sidebar on the opposite page. For best results, you should apply tape over the full length of the stock (top photo). If you don't, the rollers and cutterhead can flex the piece, resulting in an uneven cut.

Take light cuts

To adjust the depth of cut, we again recommend that you insert the sled/stock into the planer with the power off and lower the head until it just contacts the stock, Then back it off a quarter-turn, remove it, and begin planing (middle photo). As always, make sure you take light cuts; it's really important here—especially with highly figured woods, which tend to shatter when planed too thin. You'll have best luck with cuts less than $1/16$", preferably $1/32$" to $1/64$".

Easy separation

To remove the thin, fragile stock once it has been planed, drizzle acetone or lacquer thinner between the stock and the sled—it'll dissolve the tape's adhesive, and the stock will peel right off (bottom photo).

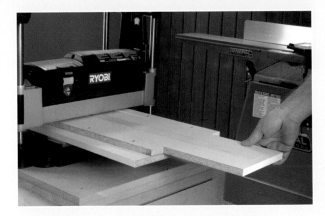

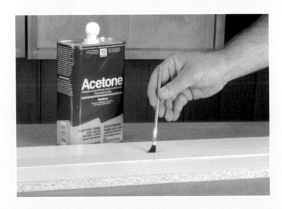

Short stock solution

Somewhere in the numerous warnings in your planer's manual is a note about minimum-length stock that can be safely planed. But there is a way you can safely plane shorter stock—just temporarily attach a pair of runners to the sides of the stock to be planed, as shown in the top photo. Just make sure that the runners are thicker than the stock. This way they'll span the space between the feed rollers, allowing the stock to pass safely past the cutterhead.

PLANER SLEDS

There are two common types of sleds used to plane thin stock on a planer: a sled that hooks onto the planer's bed, and a sled that you feed through the planer. The advantage of a hook-on sled is that you can plane multiple pieces easily. The disadvantage to this is that a hook-on sled does not support the stock to be planed as well as a feed-through sled does when the workpiece is taped to the sled.

HOOK-ON SLED

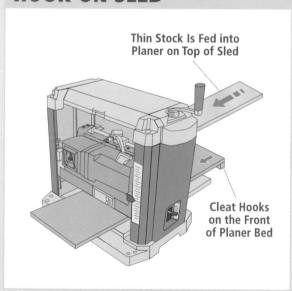

Thin Stock Is Fed into Planer on Top of Sled

Cleat Hooks on the Front of Planer Bed

FEED-THROUGH SLED

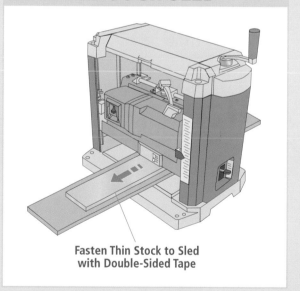

Fasten Thin Stock to Sled with Double-Sided Tape

Hook-on sled: On a hook-on sled, a cleat attached under the front edge of the sled hooks onto the bed of the planer. The stock slides on top of the sled through the planer.

Feed-through sled: With a feed-through sled, the stock is attached to the sled with double-sided tape and the sled/stock is fed through the planer.

Making Molding

Some specialty planers are capable of making molding. They combine the functions of a stationary planer and a shaper (or molder). Although not as versatile as a shaper, a planer/molder can produce an amazing array of molded profiles—everything from crown molding to tongue-and-groove flooring (see the sidebar on the opposite page). The way it works is there's a section in the middle of the cutterhead where you can remove a set of spacers and replace these with molding cutters; see the bottom right photo. (Note that wide cutters require that the knives be removed entirely.) A commercial or shop-made bed with guide rails is attached to the bed of the planer, and the stock is fed through.

Attach an auxiliary bed or guide rail system
The first step to using most planer/molders is to attach an auxiliary bed or guide rail system to the planer's bed, as shown in the top photo. Some manufacturers include a guide rail system with their planer/molders; others don't. And some sell these as an accessory. The auxiliary bed does a couple of things. First, since some molding knives cut a full profile to clean up the sides of the molding—and therefore would cut into the planer bed—an auxiliary bed is necessary to prevent damage to the blades and bed. Second, an auxiliary bed provides clamping space for adding the rails that position and guide the workpiece past the molding cutters.

Change the speed
The next step on most planer/molders is to change the feed speed. Some units have a speed lever that you can adjust. Others, like the one shown in the middle photo, require a gear swap to change speed. Slower feed rates are generally used for the molding operation to provide an improved surface finish. Note: Some manufacturers suggest that you adjust the feed roller pressure when working with wider molding. This ensures that the stock will be securely gripped while planing.

Install the cutters
With the auxiliary bed in place and the speed correct, you can insert the desired molding knives. Some planer/molders require that you remove the planer blades to do this; on other models, like the one shown here, you can leave the knives in place for molding knives 2" and less in width (for wider cutters, the planer knives must be removed). Unplug the planer, remove the dust hood to expose the knives, and use the supplied wrench to loosen the lock bars. Remove the spacer and insert the desired cutter (bottom photo); repeat for the other cutters.

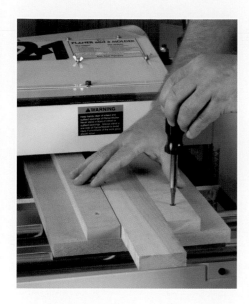

Attach the guide rails

Once you've got the cutters installed, you can reassemble the dust hood and hook it up. Next, to align and guide the stock so that it passes under the cutterhead at the appropriate point, attach guide rails to the auxiliary bed as shown in the top photo; alternatively, attach the supplied guide rail system.

Make the cut

Now you're ready to make some molding. Before you do this, it's always a good idea to run the planer for a couple of minutes to make sure the lock bars that hold the molding cutters are secure. Stop the planer, unplug it, remove the dust hood, and re-tighten the lock bars. Then read and follow the manufacturer's directions on maximum depth of cut. You'll also have best results if you pre-thickness the stock to within $1/16$" of the final thickness (middle photo). Remember: Light cuts will create a smoother finish.

MOLDING CUTTERS

There is a staggering variety of molding cutters available—everything from wide crown molding to tiny beads or even tongue-and-groove for flooring. Most manufacturers recommend using only their cutters, since they were designed specifically for their machine. Good advice. Also, most planer/molders use a set of three cutters—steer away from companies that offer single cutters and two counterweights: These can cause severe vibration and can damage your machine.

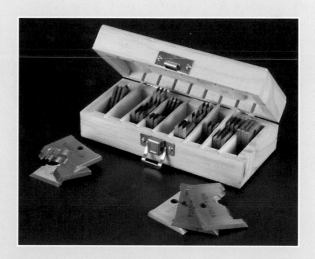

Tapered Cuts on a Planer

Occasionally you may need to cut a taper along the length or width of a post, leg, or other project part. What many woodworkers don't know is that the planer can handle these tasks with the addition of a simple shop-made sled, as illustrated in the drawings below right. The advantage that a planer offers is that you end up with accurately thicknessed parts with smooth faces—a combination that no other single stationary tool offers. Since the sled you make will be good only for tapering a specific part, it makes sense to go to the trouble of making a jig like this if you're making multiple parts—say, for example, for a set of dining room chairs. If you need only one or two tapered parts, consider tapering them on the jointer; see pages 84–87 for more on this.

Taper sled

The simple sled shown here is designed for tapering pieces from side to side. It consists of a plywood base and an angled block cut to match the desired taper angle, and it's attached to the underside of the table or sled; the angled block runs the full length of the sled. An adjustable fence is secured to the table with screws and allows you to position the workpiece from side to side to create the desired taper.

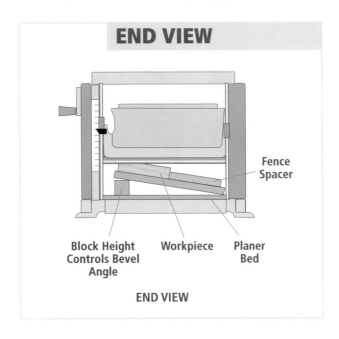

END VIEW

Fence
Spacer

Block Height
Controls Bevel
Angle

Workpiece

Planer
Bed

END VIEW

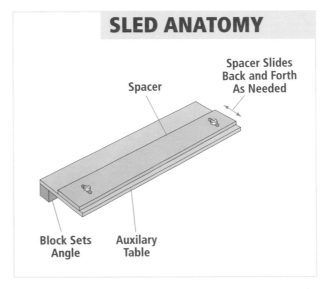

SLED ANATOMY

Spacer

Spacer Slides
Back and Forth
As Needed

Block Sets
Angle

Auxilary
Table

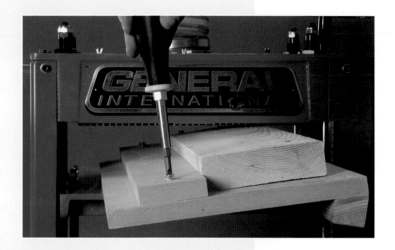

Position the stock

To use the taper sled, insert a workpiece on the sled and adjust the fence spacer as needed to create the desired taper, as shown in the top photo.

Tape to sled or use stops

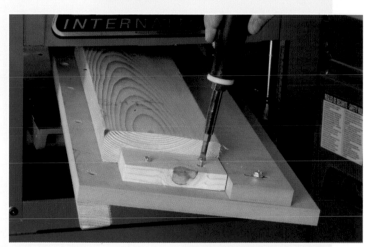

Next, to prevent the workpiece from shifting during the cut, temporarily affix the workpiece to the sled with double-sided tape. Alternatively, you can add stops to both ends of the sled to prevent the feed rollers from shifting the workpiece, as shown in the middle photo.

Plane the taper

Adjust the planer for a moderate cut, and feed the sled and workpiece through the planer as shown in the bottom photo. Continue adjusting the depth of cut and feeding the sled through the planer until the desired taper is achieved. Note that as you approach the final taper, you'll gradually be taking a wider and wider cut—so make sure to decrease the depth of cut as you go, to keep from bogging down the planer.

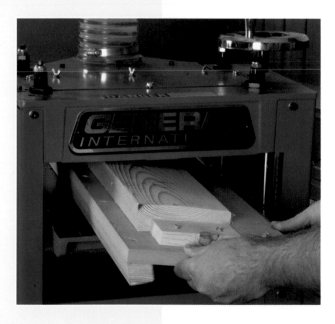

5 Shop-Made Jigs and Fixtures

Although you might not think there are a lot of jigs and fixtures that you can build for jointers and planers, there are a surprising number of them. In this chapter we'll show you how to build a stand for either a jointer or a planer, plus a push block and a thin-stock sled. There are also two additional projects that you can use with your other stationary power tools: an adjustable infeed/outfeed support and a roll-around parts cart. Each of these projects is easy to build, inexpensive, and stout enough to provide years of service.

It's the details that really count when you're building jigs and fixtures. Simple yet thoughtful details like a pull-out bin that uses a standard trash bin to make collecting and disposing of dust and chips a snap, and extensions for a planer stand that support stock yet are easily removable to take up less shop space.

Jointer Push Block

HANDLE PATTERN

Besides the built-in guard on a jointer, the number one safety device you can use when jointing wood is a push block. Although there are numerous commercially made push blocks available (see page 38), we've got along just fine with the shop-made version shown here. We prefer an all-wood version like this because if there's a slip and the push block comes in contact with the cutterhead, there's no damage. Our push block consists of a handle attached to a base that is kerfed at one end to accept a $1/4$" hardboard hook, as illustrated in the Exploded View on page 103. In use, the base presses the workpiece firmly into the bed of the jointer, and the strip of hardboard hooks over the end of the workpiece so that you can safely push it forward.

Lay out the handle pattern

To make the push block, start by tracing the full-sized pattern at right onto a piece of $3/4$" plywood. (We made a template, as we knew we'd be making more of these over time, as shown in the middle photo.) Plywood works best for a handle that's shaped like this, as the cross plies guarantee a sturdy handle. A solid-wood handle shaped like this would easily break where the grain is weakest. Note that we used premium-grade plywood, such as Baltic Birch or Apple-Ply (www.statesind.com), as it's stronger and has no voids.

Cut out the handle

Now you can cut out the shape of the handle. We did this on the band saw, but you can use a saber saw, scroll saw, or coping saw. After cutting the handle to shape, sand the curves smooth and round over the edges for a comfortable fit.

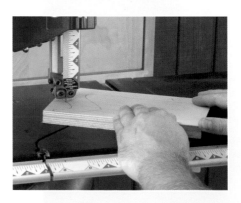

Kerf the base and add the hook

Cut a kerf in the bottom of the base roughly $1/2$" deep and slightly narrower than $1/4$" hardboard, as shown in the top photo. If you cut the kerf so that it's a bit snug, you can press-fit the hardboard strip in it as shown in the middle photo. When it gets dinged up with use, just pull it out and replace it with a fresh strip. If it's too loose, insert paper shims so that you get a press fit. If you glue the strip in, you'll have to make a new base when the hook inevitably wears out.

Attach the handle to the base

All that's left is to attach the handle to the base. Drill a couple of pilot holes in the handle and drive screws through the handle and into the base, as shown in the middle photo. Take care to size the screws so they don't poke through the bottom of the base.

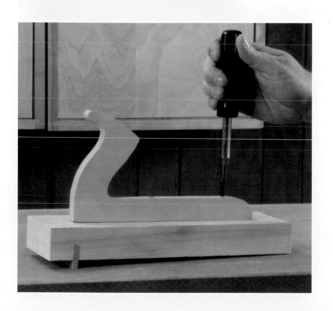

EXPLODED VIEW

Handle

Base   Hook

MATERIALS LIST

Part	Quantity	Dimensions
Handle	1	5" × 9" – $3/4$" plywood
Base	1	4" × 12" – $1\frac{1}{2}$"
Hook	1	1" × 4" – $1/4$" hardboard

Jointer Stand

A jointer stand should be heavy and sturdy, and also provide some kind of chip and dust control. The shop-made jointer stand that we designed is made of MDF (medium-density fiberboard), which weighs around 100 pounds per sheet. Since this stand uses up most of a full sheet, its weight helps dampen vibration. And the parts are glued and screwed together to create a rock-solid stand. (Note: Although the stand shown here is sized for a bench-top jointer, you can alter the dimensions to suit most stationary jointers.) We also added a pull-out bin that uses an ordinary plastic trash can to catch chips and dust; see the Exploded View on the opposite page. It slides in and out on full-extension slides to make it easy to empty. A hole in the top of the stand, along with a shop-made chute, directs chips and dust into the bin.

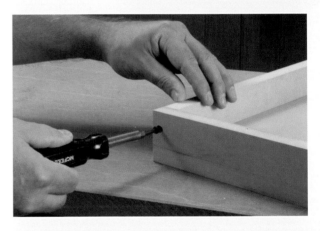

Build the pull-out tray

To make the jointer stand, begin by cutting the parts to size per the materials list on the opposite page. Next, assemble the tray that holds the plastic dust bin, as shown in the middle photo. The tray front and back are glued and screwed to the tray sides and bottom.

Attach one half of slide

The tray moves in and out on a pair of full-extension slides. Attach one half of the slides to the tray sides now, as shown in the bottom photo, following the slide installation instructions.

Rabbet the sides

To make it easier to assemble the stand, the front and back vertical edges of the sides of the stand are rabbeted to accept the front rail and back, as illustrated in the detail drawing on the bottom of page 106. We cut these rabbets on a table saw fitted with a dado blade, as shown in the top photo.

Attach the other half of the slides

Once the rabbets are cut, it's easiest now to attach the remaining half of the slides to the bottom inside edge of the sides, as shown in the middle photo.

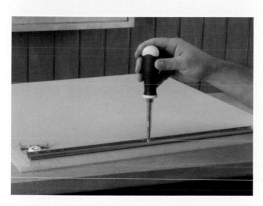

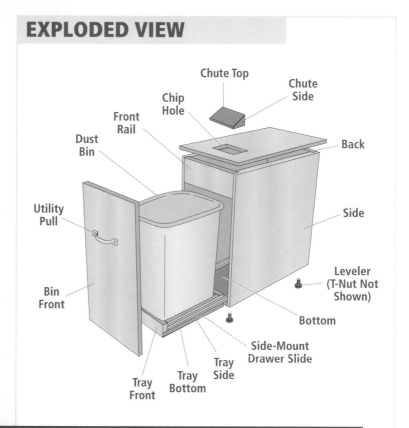

EXPLODED VIEW

Chute Top
Chute Side
Chip Hole
Front Rail
Dust Bin
Back
Utility Pull
Side
Bin Front
Leveler (T-Nut Not Shown)
Bottom
Side-Mount Drawer Slide
Tray Side
Tray Bottom
Tray Front

MATERIALS LIST

Part	Quantity	Dimensions	Part	Quantity	Dimensions
Sides	2	$23^{3}/_{4}$" × $23^{3}/_{4}$" – $^{3}/_{4}$" MDF	Dust bin	1	Rubbermaid 36-quart trash can
Front rail	1	4" × $12^{1}/_{8}$" – $^{3}/_{4}$" MDF	Slides	2	Knape & Vogt 1300 side-mount
Back	1	$12^{1}/_{8}$" × $23^{3}/_{4}$" – $^{3}/_{4}$" MDF			drawer slides (20")
Top	1	14" × 26" – $^{3}/_{4}$" MDF	Utility pull	1	$6^{1}/_{2}$"
Bottom	1	13" × $23^{3}/_{4}$" – $^{3}/_{4}$" MDF	Levelers	4	$^{5}/_{16}$" × 1"
Bin front	1	12" × $19^{3}/_{8}$" – $^{3}/_{4}$" MDF	T-nuts	4	$^{5}/_{16}$"
Tray sides	2	$1^{1}/_{2}$" × 12" – $^{3}/_{4}$" MDF	Chute sides	2	$3^{1}/_{2}$" × $3^{1}/_{2}$" – $1^{1}/_{2}$"
Tray front/back	2	$1^{1}/_{2}$" × $10^{1}/_{4}$" – $^{3}/_{4}$" MDF	Chute top	1	$5^{1}/_{2}$" × 10" – $^{1}/_{4}$" hardboard
Tray bottom	1	$10^{1}/_{4}$" × $13^{1}/_{2}$" – $^{3}/_{4}$" MDF	Levelers	4	Optional

Assemble the stand

Now you can assemble the stand. Apply glue to the edges of the back and front rail, and slip these into the rabbets in the sides. Apply clamps and allow to dry overnight, as shown in the top photo. Then remove the clamps, drill pilot holes, and screw the sides to the back and front rail. At the same time, you can attach the bin front to the tray with glue and screws; drive the screws through the tray front and into the bin front.

Add the bottom and top

The next step is to attach the bottom and top to the stand with glue and screws (middle photo) and then lay out and cut an opening in the top to direct chips into the bin. Position the jointer on the top and lay out the hole as shown in the bottom photo. Then drill a hole for a saber saw blade and cut the opening. Note: If your jointer has its motor mounted below, you'll need to modify the stand—cut an opening in the top for the drive belt and add a support below for the motor. Depending on the placement of the motor, you may need to resize the trash bin and pull-out tray or eliminate it completely, replacing it with a baffle to direct chips to a dust port. This is also the best time to add levelers to the bottom if desired.

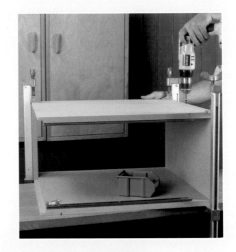

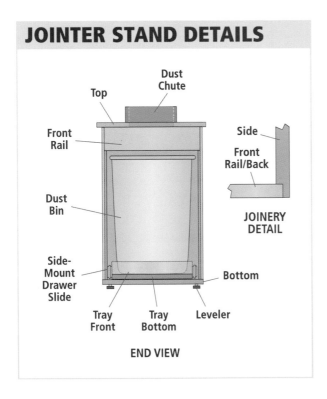

JOINTER STAND DETAILS

Dust Chute

Top

Front Rail

Side

Front Rail/Back

JOINERY DETAIL

Dust Bin

Side-Mount Drawer Slide

Bottom

Tray Front

Tray Bottom

Leveler

END VIEW

Attach the jointer

With the stand and pull-out bin complete, you can attach the jointer. Position the jointer on top of the stand so that the end aligns with the opening that you made in the top. Then mark and drill mounting holes. Attach the jointer to the top with carriage bolts, nuts, and lock washers, as shown in the top photo. If your jointer has the motor mounted below, feed the drive belt up through the opening and attach it to the pulley on the jointer.

Build the dust chute

Depending on the location of the dust chute on your jointer, you may or may not need to make a shop-made chute to help direct chips and dust from the jointer into the pull-out dust bin. The bench-top jointer shown here requires such a chute. It's just a pair of wood wedges and a $1/4"$ hardboard top (the top and bottom edges are beveled to match the 45-degree angle of the wedges).

Attach the chute and bin pull

Finally, attach the shop-made chute to the jointer stand with screws from underneath, as shown in the bottom left photo. Then attach a pull to the bin front as shown in the bottom right photo.

Thin-Stock Sled

Although all planer manufacturers provide mechanical limits on their machines to keep woodworkers from planing stock below a recommended thickness (typically $1/4$"), projects often call for stock that's thinner. Since most woodworkers aren't interested in paying premium prices for thin stock, they elect to make it themselves. The most common way to get around the mechanical limits or stops on a planer to "raise" the bed closer to the cutterhead via some type of sled. Although this is a common practice, it's important that you understand that thin stock can and often will explode in the planer with this method. If you choose to try this, make sure you don't stand directly behind or in front of the planer. Wear safety glasses, take thin cuts, and make sure your knives are sharp.

There are two common ways to plane thin stock on a planer: a sled that hooks onto the planer's bed, and a sled that you feed through the planer. The advantage of a hook-on sled is that you can plane multiple pieces easily. The disadvantage to this is that a hook-on sled does not support the stock to be planed as well as a feed-through sled when the workpiece is taped to the sled. The thin stock sled shown here can handle either technique. It consists of a base and cleat, a pair of angled runners, and a sled, as shown in the Exploded View on the opposite page. You can build just the base and cleat as a hook-on sled, where you pass the pieces directly through the planer. Or add the runners that guide the sliding table (with the workpiece attached via double-sided tape) at an angle to produce a shearing cut.

Attach the cleat to the base

To build the thin-stock sled, cut the pieces to size per the materials list on the opposite page. Note that we used melamine, as its smooth surface allows the workpiece (or sled) to slide with minimal friction. Attach the cleat to the base as shown in the bottom photo.

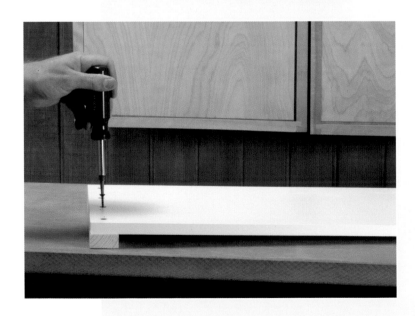

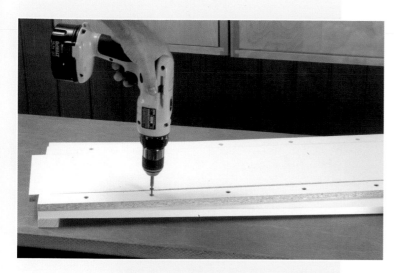

Attach the angled runners (if desired)

Next, attach the runners to the base at an angle (if desired), as shown in the top photo. The best way to do this is to sandwich the sliding table between the runners as you screw them to the base.

Attach the stock to the sled

To use the thin-stock sled, insert the base in your planer and then attach the stock to the sliding table with double-sided tape. Adjust the planer for a light cut and plane, continuing until the desired thickness is reached (see pages 94–95 for more on planning thin stock).

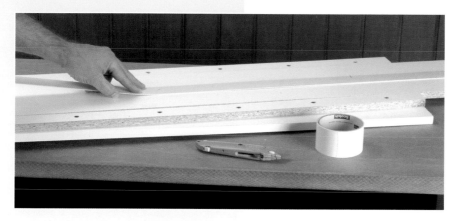

EXPLODED VIEW

Sliding Table

Cleat

Base

Runner

MATERIALS LIST

Part	Quantity	Dimensions
Base	1	12" × 36" – 3/4" melamine
Cleat	1	1 1/2" × 12" – 3/4" pine
Runners	2	1 1/2" × 36" – 3/4" melamine
Sliding table	1	6 3/4" × 48" – 3/4" melamine

Planer Stand

The biggest problem with planers is their tendency to snipe the ends of boards. The simplest way to reduce snipe is to fully support the workpiece as it enters and exits the planer. Although most planers come with infeed and outfeed tables or rollers to support a workpiece, they're typically fairly short so that they don't take up valuable shop space. This often forces you to set up some kind of auxiliary support to prevent or reduce snipe. We've always found this a hassle, so we designed this stand with extensions that not only fully support the workpiece but also can be easily removed when not needed.

The stand itself is very sturdy, as the rails join to the legs via large single dovetails, as illustrated in the Exploded View drawing on the opposite page. The two halves of the stand are spanned by end rails that are held in place with threaded rods. A double-layer of MDF serves as the top—all in all, a stout, heavy stand. To provide maximum support without sagging, we employed metal shelf brackets in our extensions. The extensions connect to the stand by way of a pair of beveled cleats—one of which is adjustable for fine-tuning the extension's position. Note: If your planer's extensions are adequate, you can build the stand sans extensions.

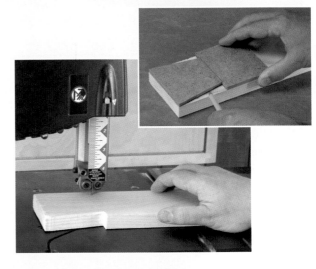

Lay out and cut the dovetailed rails

To build the stand, start by cutting the parts to size per the materials list. Then use the dovetail detail shown on page 112 to lay out the dovetails on the rail ends, as shown in the middle inset photo. (We made a template following the drawing, to make layout easy.) Then cut the dovetails (middle photo).

Cut the angled spacers

The legs are built up from three layers of $3/4"$ MDF, along with the dovetailed ends of the rails. The inner layer is made up of spacers angled to match the dovetails; see the drawing on page 112. The middle spacer is angled on each end, and the bottom spacer is angled on one end only. Cut these on the table saw (as shown in the bottom photo) or on a miter saw.

EXPLODED VIEW

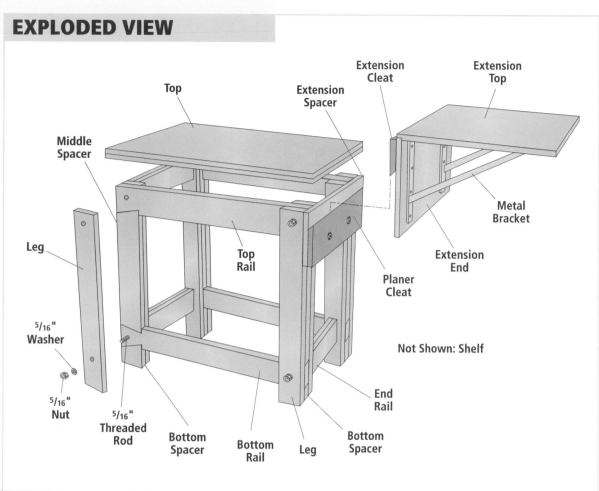

Top

Extension Spacer

Extension Cleat

Extension Top

Middle Spacer

Leg

Top Rail

Metal Bracket

Extension End

Planer Cleat

5/16" Washer

5/16" Nut

5/16" Threaded Rod

Bottom Spacer

Bottom Rail

Leg

Bottom Spacer

End Rail

Not Shown: Shelf

MATERIALS LIST

Part	Quantity	Dimensions
Legs	8	3" × 28" – 3/4" MDF
Middle spacers	4	3" × 17 1/4" – 3/4" MDF
Bottom spacers	4	3" × 5 1/4" – 3/4" MDF
Top/bottom rails	4	3 1/2" × 28" – 3/4" pine
End rails	4	3 1/2" × 13 1/2" – 1 1/2" pine*
Shelf	1	(optional, cut to fit)
Threaded rods	4	5/16" × 19"
Washers	8	5/16"
Nuts	8	5/16"
Top	1	19 1/2" × 20 1/2" – 1 1/2" MDF†
Extension spacers	2	7" × 18" – 3/4" MDF

Part	Quantity	Dimensions
Planer cleats	2	6" × 18" – 3/4" MDF
Extension cleats	2	4 3/4" × 18" – 3/4" MDF
Extension tops	2	18" × 19" – 3/4" MDF
Extension ends	2	12" × 19 1/2" – 3/4" MDF
Brackets	4	Stanley #25-7550/795 (16" × 10")
Carriage bolts	4	1/4" × 2"
Wing nuts	4	1/4"
Washers	4	1/4"

* Each end rail is two 3/4"-thick pieces glued together.
† Top is glued up of two 3/4" pieces of MDF.

Glue up the leg assemblies

Once you've got all the spacers cut, you can assemble the stand. This is best done in layers. Start by gluing the top rail to a pair of legs, making sure that they are perpendicular to each other. Next add the middle spacers, followed by the bottom rail and bottom spacers. Then glue on the outer leg layer as shown in the top photo; repeat for the remaining leg assembly.

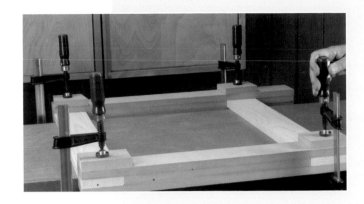

Groove the end rails

The leg assemblies are connected via the end rails. A $5/16$" threaded rod passes through centered grooves cut into the rail pieces; see the detail drawing below. We cut these grooves on the table saw, as shown in the middle photo.

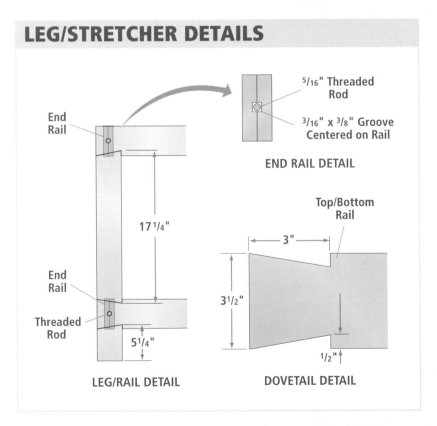

LEG/STRETCHER DETAILS

End Rail

$5/16$" Threaded Rod

$3/16$" x $3/8$" Groove Centered on Rail

END RAIL DETAIL

End Rail

Threaded Rod

17 1/4"

5 1/4"

LEG/RAIL DETAIL

Top/Bottom Rail

3"

3 1/2"

1/2"

DOVETAIL DETAIL

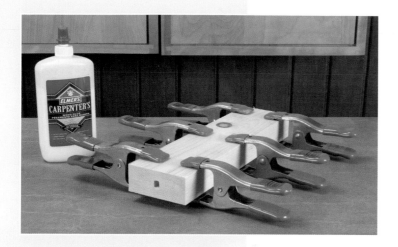

Glue up the end rails

With the grooves cut in all four sets of end rails, go ahead and glue the pairs of end rails together, as shown in the top photo. Take care to keep glue away from the grooves. Set the rails aside and allow the glue to dry overnight.

Assemble the stand

Now you can assemble the stand. Start by drilling holes in the leg assemblies for the threaded rod, as shown in the detail drawing on page 112. Then thread the rods through the rails and push the protruding ends of the rods through the holes in the leg assemblies. Slip on washers and nuts and tighten the nuts to cinch the end rails between the leg assemblies. Note: If you want to add a shelf, now is the time to cut one to fit and screw it to the end and bottom rails.

Add the top

The top is just two layers of 3/4" MDF. Cut the layers to size, and glue and screw them together. Then center the top on the stand from side to side and from front to back, and secure it to the stand with screws, as shown in the bottom photo.

Make the extension top

If you're going to build the extensions, start by making the top. Cut a rabbet on one end as detailed in the drawing below. Then attach a piece of oversized plastic laminate to the top with contact cement and trim the laminate to match the top, using a flush-trim bit, as shown in the top photo. Follow this up with a chamfer bit to relieve the edges.

Assemble the extension

Next, glue the extension end in the rabbet that you cut in the extension stop, and then attach a pair of metal shelf brackets to the underside of the extension as shown in the middle photo; repeat for the other extension. Allow the glue to dry overnight.

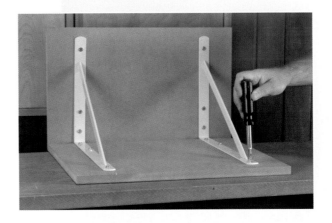

EXTENSION DETAILS

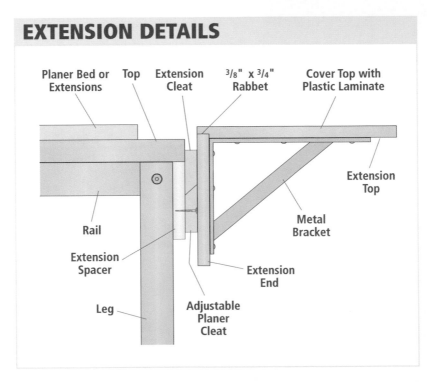

Planer Bed or Extensions

Top

Extension Cleat

3/8" x 3/4" Rabbet

Cover Top with Plastic Laminate

Extension Top

Rail

Metal Bracket

Extension Spacer

Extension End

Leg

Adjustable Planer Cleat

Attach the extension cleats

Now you can bevel-rip the cleats to size (the bevel is 45 degrees). Then attach the extension cleats to your extensions as shown in the top photo. These are glued and screwed to the back face of the extension ends. Where you attach these cleats, along with the planer cleats, will depend on your planer. Set your planer on the stand and set a 4-foot level on the planer bed. Position the extension so the top is flush with the bottom of the level. This will give you a rough approximation as to where the cleats need to be installed.

Attach the spacers and planer cleats

The planer cleats attach to extension spacers mounted on the ends of the stand directly under the top, as shown in the drawing on page 114. Cut and attach the extension spacers to the stand as shown in the middle photo. Then clamp the planer cleats to the extension spacers and drill a pair of $1/4$" holes through the cleats and spacers for the $1/4$" carriage bolts that secure the cleat to the spacer. Remove the clamps, and counterbore the holes in the cleats so the heads of the carriage bolts will sit below the face of the cleat. Then elongate the holes in the extension spacers to form slots for adjusting the planer cleats; see below. Attach the planer cleats to the extension spacers with $1/4$" carriage bolts, washers, and wing nuts.

Adjust the extension

Mount the extension and then adjust it up or down as needed until it's aligned with the bed of the planer, as shown in the bottom photo. Fully tighten the wing nuts. If you plan on leaving the extensions in place, consider driving screws through the extension spacer and planer cleat into the extension end for added support.

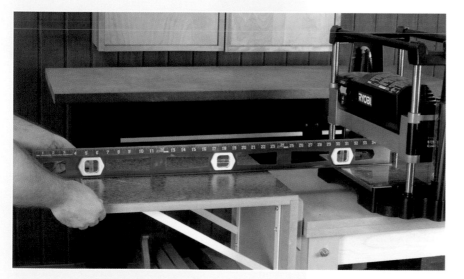

Infeed/Outfeed Support

Just about every planer and jointer can use some help supporting long or heavy stock—even long-bed jointers and planers with wide infeed and outfeed tables or rollers. That's where infeed/outfeed support comes in. Yes, you can buy metal versions of these, but quality units are expensive and typically have rollers. And rollers not perfectly parallel to your jointer or planer will tend to skew the workpiece as it passes over the roller. The shop-made infeed/outfeed support shown here offers fully adjustable support. What's more, it employs a non-roller rub strip that can't skew a workpiece. This strip is made from ultra-high-molecular-weight polyethylene (UHMW) to provide near-frictionless support. UHMW can be purchased from most mail-order woodworking companies, including Woodcraft (www.woodcraft.com), in a variety of sizes and thicknesses.

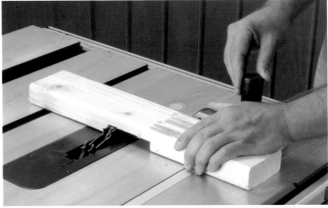

Our infeed/outfeed support consists of a front and back arm attached to feet that sport angled levelers. A sliding arm attaches to the front arm via a carriage bolt and wing nut that allows the arm to slide up or down as needed. The sliding arm terminates with a support that holds a UHMW rub strip; see the Exploded View on the opposite page.

Cut the half-laps
To build the support, start by cutting the parts to size per the materials list on the opposite page. Then with a dado blade installed in the table saw, cut half-laps on one end of the front and back arm and centered on the feet, as detailed in the drawing on page 119 and shown in the middle photo.

Shape the feet
Transfer the layout for the feet shown on page 119 to the feet. Then drill holes as noted and cut the feet to shape as shown in the bottom photo.

Assemble the arms

Now you can assemble the front and back arms. Apply glue to both faces of the half-laps, position the parts, and apply clamps as shown in the top photo. Allow the glue to dry overnight.

EXPLODED VIEW

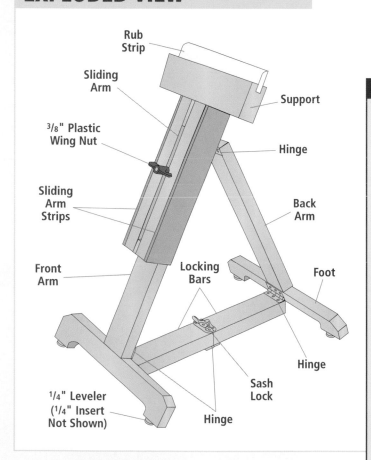

Rub Strip

Sliding Arm

3/8" Plastic Wing Nut

Sliding Arm Strips

Front Arm

Support

Hinge

Back Arm

Foot

Locking Bars

1/4" Leveler (1/4" Insert Not Shown)

Hinge

Sash Lock

Hinge

MATERIALS LIST		
Part	**Quantity**	**Dimensions**
Feet	2	$3^{1}/_{2}$" × 18" – $1^{1}/_{2}$"
Front arm	1	$3^{1}/_{2}$" × 30" – $1^{1}/_{2}$"
Back arm	1	$3^{1}/_{2}$" × $22^{1}/_{2}$" – $1^{1}/_{2}$"
Sliding arm	1	$3^{1}/_{2}$" × 18" – $1^{1}/_{2}$"*
Support	1	$3^{1}/_{2}$" × 12" $1^{1}/_{2}$"
Rub strip	1	3" × 12" – $^{1}/_{2}$"
		UHMW plastic
Sliding arm strips	2	$2^{1}/_{2}$" × $14^{1}/_{2}$" – $^{1}/_{4}$"
		hardboard
Locking bars	2	$3^{1}/_{2}$" × 10" – $1^{1}/_{2}$"
Hinges	4	2" × $3^{1}/_{2}$"
Sash lock	1	two-piece
Inserts	4	$^{1}/_{4}$"
Levelers	4	$^{1}/_{4}$", swivel
Plastic wing nut	1	$^{3}/_{8}$" threads
Washer	1	$^{3}/_{8}$"
Carriage bolt	1	$^{3}/_{8}$" × 4"

* Glued up from four pieces; see text.

Glue up the sliding arm

A groove in the sliding arm allows it to move up and down on the front arm. Instead of routing this groove, it's easier to glue up the arm from four pieces, as detailed in the drawing on page 119. Cut the sides and a pair of spacers as noted, and glue the pieces together as shown in the top photo. Allow the glue to dry overnight.

Cut the half-lap and glue up the support

Now you can cut the half-laps that join the sliding arm to the support. Here again we did this on the table saw, fitted with a dado blade, as shown in the middle left photo. Then glue the support to the sliding arm as shown in the middle right photo.

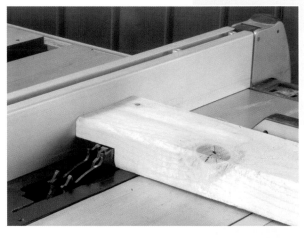

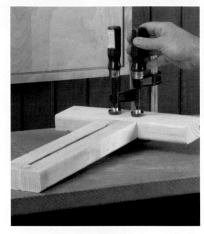

Cut the groove for the rub strip

The rub strip fits into a groove cut along the length of the support. Install a dado blade in your table saw to match the thickness of the rub strip, and cut the 1"-deep groove as shown in the bottom photo.

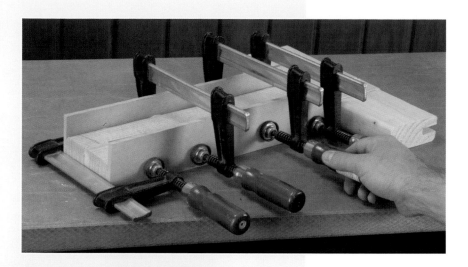

Add the sliding arm strips

The next step is to glue the sliding arm to the support. When dry, attach the sliding arm strips to the sides of the sliding arm, using glue and clamps, as shown in the top photo. These strips keep the sliding arm centered on the front arm as it slides up and down.

Attach the rub strip

Before you attach the rub strip to the support, round over the top front edge of the strip. You want a full profile roundover here, so use a $1/2$" roundover bit. The most secure way to attach the rub strip to the support is with epoxy. To ensure a good bond, it's best to first rough up the bottom edge and faces of the rub strip with sandpaper to provide a purchase for the epoxy. Mix up some 5-minute epoxy, apply it in the groove in the support, and insert the rub strip as shown in the middle photo.

SUPPORT DETAILS

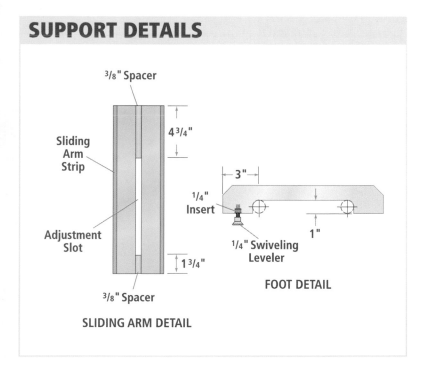

$3/8$" Spacer

Sliding Arm Strip

$4 3/4$"

$1/4$" Insert

3"

Adjustment Slot

$1/4$" Swiveling Leveler

1"

$1 3/4$"

$3/8$" Spacer

SLIDING ARM DETAIL

FOOT DETAIL

Attach the hinges

Our infeed/outfeed support is designed to knock down for easy storage when not in use. The support employs four hinges for this: one that joins the front arm to the back arm, one that connects the two halves of the locking bar, and two that connect the bottom of the front and back arms to the locking bar, as shown in the Exploded View on page 117. Start by attaching the hinges to the locking bar: one at the joint and two on the ends, as shown in the top photo.

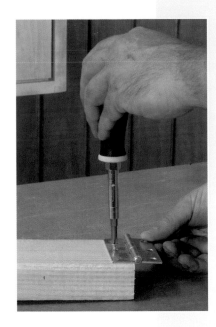

Assemble the infeed/outfeed support

Next, attach a hinge to the top inside faces of the front and back arm as shown in the middle photo.

Attach the locking bar

Position the infeed/outfeed support on a level surface and place the locking bar between the legs as shown in the bottom photo. Now you can secure the hinges on the ends of the locking bar to the front and back arm. Make sure to drill pilot holes before installing the screws. A self-centering drill bit (sometimes referred to as a Vix bit) makes this a simple task.

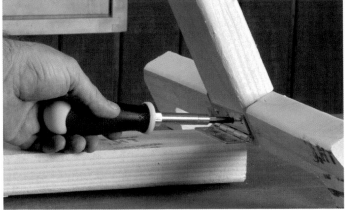

Add the sash lock

Now add a sash lock to the top of the locking bar where the two halves butt up against each other, as shown in the top photo. In the closed position, this will lock the locking bar in place so that it cannot fold up. In the open position, it allows the locking bar to fold up for storing the infeed/outfeed support.

Assemble the sliding arm/support

All that left is to attach the sliding arm onto the front arm. To do this, place the sliding arm over the front arm so it's in its lowest position, and clamp it in place as shown in the middle photo. Then drill a $3/8$" hole through the top of the slot in the sliding arm through the front arm for the carriage bolt that secures the two parts, as shown in the bottom photo. Pass the carriage bolt through the back of the front arm and through the slot in the sliding arm. Slip on a washer, and thread on the wing nut. Remove the clamps and test the action of the sliding arm.

Roll-Around Parts Cart

One thing that many woodworking shops have in common is that there's never enough horizontal storage space. One of the biggest challenges to preparing wood for a project is finding someplace to set the parts down as you're surfacing them. A parts cart, like the one shown here, is the answer. It provides plenty of space to hold parts, including built-in shelves; and it's mobile so that you can wheel it around from the lumber rack to the jointer and planer and then to the bench or table saw. And if you modify its height to match the height of one or more of your stationary power tools, it can even serve as an infeed or outfeed support, since all four of the wheels can be locked to solidly hold the stand in place. The top is covered with 1/4" melamine or plastic laminate not only to protect it from heavy use, but also to create a slick surface for sliding parts on and off. Covering the top with laminate makes the cart useful as a small assembly table as well, since glue can be scraped off easily.

Cut grooves and rabbets in the sides

To build the parts cart, start by cutting the parts to size per the materials list on the opposite page. Then cut the grooves and rabbets in the inside faces of the sides as detailed in the drawing below. We did this on the table saw fitted with a dado blade, as shown in the bottom photo. Note that these are sized to match the combined thickness of the shelves plus the laminate or melamine that you're using.

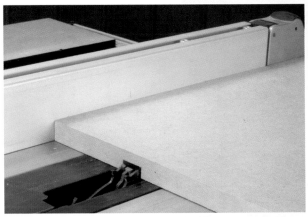

PARTS CART DETAILS

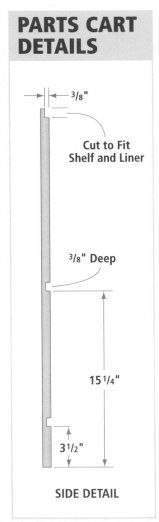

3/8"

Cut to Fit Shelf and Liner

3/8" Deep

15 1/4"

3 1/2"

SIDE DETAIL

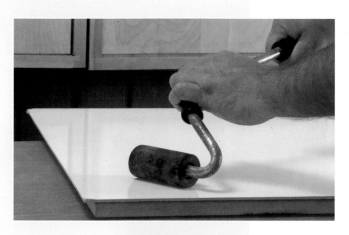

Attach laminate to the shelves

The next step is to attach plastic laminate or the melamine shelf liners to the tops of the shelves. In either case, start by cutting the laminate or melamine oversized and attaching it to the shelves with contact cement, as shown in the top photo. Then use a laminate trimmer or router fitted with a flush-trim bit to remove the excess, as shown in the middle photo.

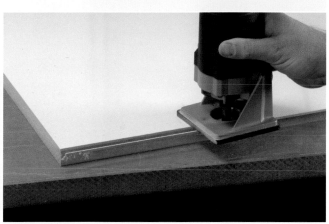

EXPLODED VIEW

Cross Dowel

Shelf Liner

Shelf

Shelf Bracket

Caster Cleat

Swivel Caster

Side

MATERIALS LIST

Part	Quantity	Dimensions
Sides	2	28" × 28" – $3/4$" MDF
Shelves	3	$19^1/4$" × 28" – $3/4$" MDF
Shelf liners	3	$19^1/4$" × 28" – $1/4$" melamine
Shelf brackets	6	$3^1/2$" × $18^1/2$" – $3/4$" pine
Cross dowels	12	3"-long, $3/8$"-dia.
Caster cleats	2	$3^1/2$" × $18^1/2$" – $1^1/2$"
Casters	4	3" locking swivel

Assemble the cart

To assemble the cart, start by applying glue to the grooves and rabbets in the sides. Then assemble the parts and apply clamps, as shown in the top photo, taking care to measure diagonals and compare for square. If the measurements are the same, the assembly is square; if not, adjust clamp position until they are. Allow the glue to dry overnight.

Add the braces

Remove the clamps from the assembly and prepare the shelf cleats by installing cross dowels as described in the sidebar on the opposite page. Apply glue to the top edge of a shelf support, and clamp it to the underside of a shelf. Then drill holes though the sides and into the supports. Drive screws through the sides and into the supports as shown in the middle photo.

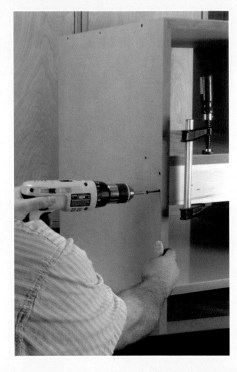

Add the wheel cleats

Flip the cart upside down and install the wheel cleats. Apply glue to the outside edge, and clamp a cleat in place against a bottom shelf support. Then drill holes through the sides and into the cleats. Drive screws through the sides and into the cleats as shown in the bottom photo.

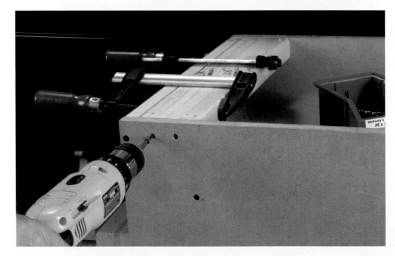

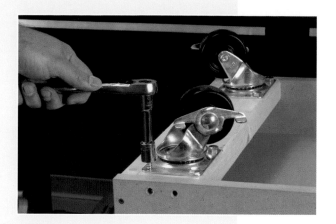

Install the casters

Finally, mount the casters to the wheel cleats. Position each caster at the ends of the cleats, and mark the mounting-hole locations. Drill pilot holes, and secure each caster with lag screws as shown in the top photo.

CROSS DOWELS

Although you could simply screw the sides to the shelf brackets, the screws won't have any holding power as they screw into end grain. Cross dowels are a nifty way to give the screws something to "bite" into and pull the parts securely together, as shown in the drawing below.

DOWEL DETAILS

Cross Dowel

#8 x 2 FH Woodscrew

TOP VIEW ← 7/8" →

1"

3/4"

Cross Dowel

SIDE VIEW

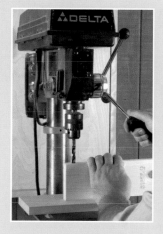

Drill the dowel holes. Start by drilling centered, 1/2"-diameter holes 7/8" in from the ends of the shelf brackets on the underside of each piece—roughly 3" deep. You can do this with a portable electric drill, but a drill press will drill a truly vertical hole.

Glue in the dowels. Then cut 3" lengths of 1/2" dowel and glue them into the holes as shown, taking care to orient the grain as shown in the drawing at left. You want the dowel grain to be perpendicular to the screw so the screw won't split the dowel.

6 Maintenance and Repair

The two tools that can have a huge impact on the precision of your woodworking—the jointer and the planer—are often the most ignored in terms of maintenance. The main reason for this reluctance has to do with the widely held perception that they're extremely difficult to adjust. This just isn't true. In most cases, the adjustments are fairly simple to make. Granted, most require a good bit of patience, but the procedures aren't complicated. In this chapter, we'll start with cleaning, inspecting, and lubricating jointers and planers. Then on to how to adjust and maintain tables, beds, extensions, and knives. We've included knife-adjusting methods ranging from the low-tech stick method to using a dial indicator or a magnetic holding jig.

The primary tools for keeping a jointer or planer in tip-top condition are the jigs used to accurately position the knives. These range from simple sight guides to holders with built-in magnets.

Jointer Anatomy

Regardless of its size and capabilities, every jointer has a base that
holds the cutterhead, an infeed
and outfeed table, and some type
of fence, as illustrated in the
drawing at right. The infeed and
outfeed tables of a jointer are
attached to the base on inclined
planes (ways) to allow for adjustment. As you turn the infeed
handwheel, the table slides up
and down on the inclined ways
to regulate the depth of cut.
On most jointers, the ways are
dovetail-shaped, with the female
half on the base and the male
half in the underside of the table.
The tables are held in place with
gib screws and locknuts set into
the side of the tables; see the
drawing at right. These screws
thread into the gibs, which are
flat metal bars located between
the mating surfaces of the ways.

Safety note: Whenever you work on a planer or
jointer, always unplug the machine first and exercise
extreme caution when working around the knives—
these are incredibly sharp and can slice through
your fingertips in the blink of an eye.

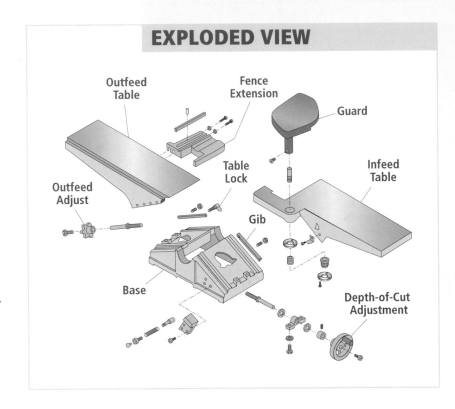

EXPLODED VIEW

Outfeed Table

Fence Extension

Guard

Table Lock

Outfeed Adjust

Infeed Table

Gib

Base

Depth-of-Cut Adjustment

Jointer Cleaning and Inspection

In order for a jointer to make a precise cut, the infeed and outfeed tables need to be kept clean and free from debris, and the jointer should be routinely inspected for wear and tear.

Clean the tables

Hooking up your jointer to some form of dust collection is the best way to keep your jointer clean. Even still, it's important to wipe down the tables periodically with a clean cloth, as shown in the top photo. If your tables are protected with wax (page 132), this is all it should take. If not, you may need to wet the cloth with mineral spirits or lacquer thinner to remove any gum or pitch deposits.

Blow out the motor

Unless your jointer's motor is the totally enclosed fan-cooled type, it's a good idea to periodically blow out the motor to prevent chips and dust from building up on the windings and/or interfering with the cooling fins, as shown in the middle photo. When sawdust builds up on the windings, it acts to insulate the wires and keeps unwanted heat in. And heat buildup can result in premature motor failure.

Blow out the cutterhead and guard pivot

At the same time that you blow out the motor, go ahead and give the cutterhead and guard pivot a blast of air to clean out any built-up dust and chips, as shown in the bottom photo. Keeping these areas clean will help them spin and pivot more reliably.

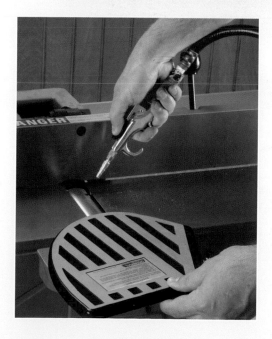

Check the tables for flatness

Many woodworkers think that just because a tool is made from cast iron, it will be perfectly flat and will always stay that way. Not true. Cast iron that's improperly cured can and does warp or twist over time. That's why it's important to periodically check your tables to make sure they're flat. Lay an accurate straightedge along the length of each table as shown in the top photo. Then check for gaps with a feeler gauge. Any gap over 0.010" should be addressed. A reliable machine shop can regrind the surfaces flat; some tool manufacturers also provide this service.

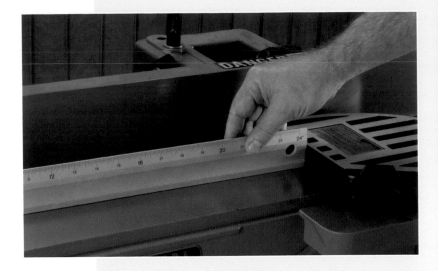

In addition to checking to make sure your tables are flat, you should also check them periodically for twist. The easiest way to do this is with a pair of shop-made "winding sticks," as shown in the middle photo. These sticks are nothing more than like-sized blocks of wood that are machined flat and square. Place the sticks on each table an equal distance from the ends. Then sight along the sticks at a low angle to check for twist. If you detect a twist (as illustrated in the bottom drawing), you may be able to fix this (see pages 136–137); otherwise the table will need to be reground.

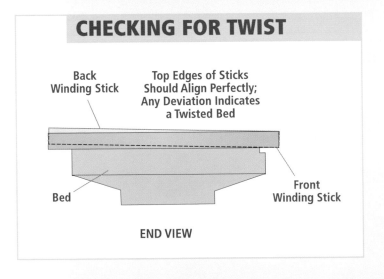

CHECKING FOR TWIST

Back Winding Stick

Top Edges of Sticks Should Align Perfectly; Any Deviation Indicates a Twisted Bed

Bed

Front Winding Stick

END VIEW

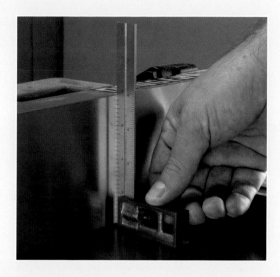

Check the fence

It's also a good idea to check to make sure the face of your jointer's fence is perpendicular to the tables. To check alignment, just butt a try square up against the fence as shown in the top photo. There shouldn't be any gap between the square and the fence or the table. If there is, you'll need to correct this by adjusting the fence and its 90-degree stop. Check your owner's manual for adjustment procedure.

Check the guard

Your guard must cover the knives, regardless of the position of the fence—move the fence to both extremes to ensure that it does, as shown in the middle photo. Make sure to pull it away from the fence at both extremes to be sure the spring pivots it fully closed. If it doesn't close fully or is slow in closing, you'll need to adjust the tension. This is usually just a matter of lifting the guard off the jointer, tightening the recoil spring, and reinserting it in the jointer; check your owner's manual for specifics.

Check the drive belt

You should also routinely check the drive belt for wear and tear and tension. One of the quickest ways to check for wear is to slide your fingers gently down the edges of the belt. If you detect fraying or cracks, it's time for a new belt. Tension can checked by pinching the belt together as shown in the bottom photo. You're looking for a total deflection of around $1/2$" or so; check your owner's manual for specifics and adjust if necessary.

Jointer Lubrication

The best time to lubricate your jointer is right after you've cleaned and inspected it (pages 129–131). Lubrication points and the recommended lubricants are illustrated in the top drawing.

Infeed and outfeed tables

Call us old-fashioned, but we still prefer to use good old paste wax for the jointer tables. Although there are numerous "high-tech" spray-ons available, we've always that found paste wax works just fine. After you've cleaned the tables (page 129), wipe on a light coat of wax as shown in the bottom photo. After it has dried to a haze, buff the surface with a clean, dry cloth. It's also a good idea to wax the tables before and after a large project where the jointer gets a lot of use.

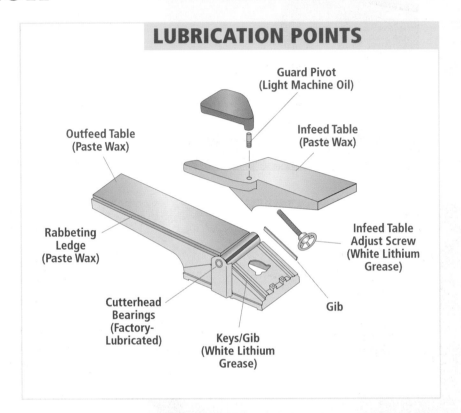

LUBRICATION POINTS

Guard Pivot (Light Machine Oil)

Outfeed Table (Paste Wax)

Infeed Table (Paste Wax)

Rabbeting Ledge (Paste Wax)

Infeed Table Adjust Screw (White Lithium Grease)

Cutterhead Bearings (Factory-Lubricated)

Gib

Keys/Gib (White Lithium Grease)

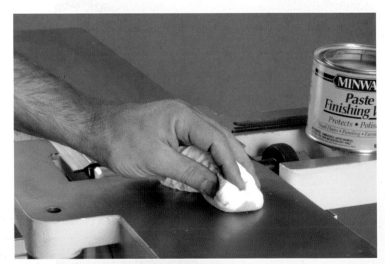

Fence pivot

Although most woodworkers do a good job of keeping their jointer's tables clean and lubricated, they often overlook the fence—in particular, the pivot points. That's because not everyone tilts their fence regularly. Without periodic lubrication, the pivot point can rust and seize up; then when you do want to tilt the fence, you've got a problem. Apply a few drops of light machine oil at least twice a year to the pivot points (as shown in the top photo), and more often if you frequently tilt the fence.

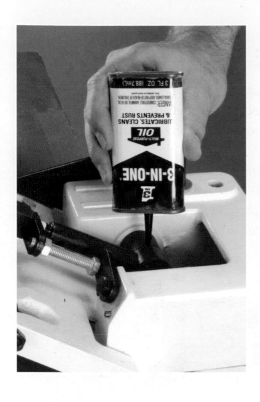

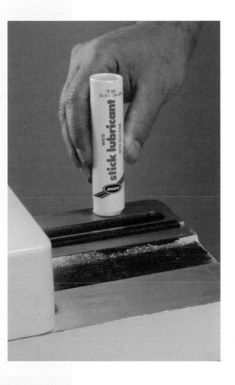

Fence slide

Unlike the tilting mechanism, the fence itself is generally adjusted regularly by sliding it back and forth across the width of the jointer to position a workpiece. Not only is it constantly adjusted, but the sliding surfaces are exposed to shop dust and grime. That's why it's important to clean off the sliding surfaces regularly and apply a light coat of grease, as shown in the middle photo. We've found that white lithium grease works well for this.

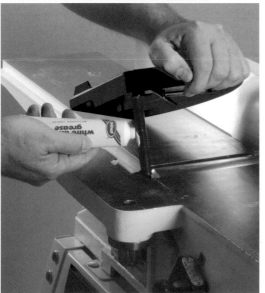

Guard

You should also periodically lubricate the pivot point for your guard, as shown in the bottom photo. Light machine oil works well here, as does white lithium grease. Just apply either sparingly, as both attract dust that can quickly bond to the lubricant, forming a thick goo.

LUBRICATING THE INFEED TABLE

If you find that it's difficult to raise and lower your infeed table, odds are that the lubricant has dried out and needs to be refreshed. Before you go about this major task, consider trying the quick fix described below. Note that this is only a temporary fix; eventually you'll need to remove the infeed table as described below and re-lubricate.

Quick fix. If you don't have the time to remove the infeed table and lubricate it, try spraying some penetrating oil (like WD-40) onto the slides as you work the table up and down, as shown in the top photo. At the same time, spray the oil on the treads of the adjusting screw connected to the handwheel. With luck, the oil will rejuvenate the dried grease.

Lock the table in place. Jointer tables are heavy—the infeed table on a standard 8" jointer weighs around 100 pounds. So make sure to have a helper on hand to help lift, remove, and replace the table.

Before you disconnect the height-adjusting screw (see below), it's imperative that you fully lock the table in place by tightening the table lock, as shown in the top right photo. **Safety note:** If the table isn't locked in place, it can slide off the base onto the floor as soon as you unbolt the block that captures the height-adjusting screw. Also, some jointers may tip when you remove one table; so position a support under the remaining table to prevent this from happening.

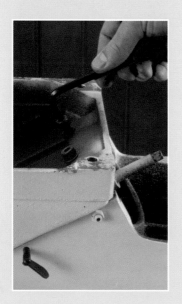

Disconnect the height-adjusting screw. The bolts that hold the height-adjusting screw block in place are typically under the base of the jointer and can be accessed only from below, as shown in the bottom left photo. In some cases you'll have to remove the jointer from the stand to access these (as shown here).

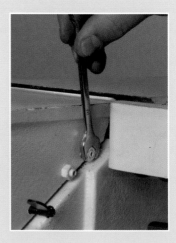

Loosen the gib-adjusting screws. Before you can remove the table, you'll need to loosen the gib-adjusting screws a turn or so, as shown in the bottom right photo. As soon as you loosen these, the only thing holding the table in place is the table lock.

Remove the table. Have your helper hold one side of the table as you hold the other side and release the table lock. At this point the table should slide off the base easily, as shown in the top photo. Which way you have to slide the table will depend on the jointer—some slide down; others slide up and over the cutterhead. Set the table upside down (with the gibs facing up) on a padded surface.

Remove the old grease. Now you have full access to the screw threads, gibs, and dovetailed ways. Use rags dipped in solvent to remove the old grease, as shown in the middle left photo. When the grease has been removed, check all surfaces for burrs and remove any you find, using a flat mill file or a scrap block wrapped with emery cloth (as shown in the middle right photo).

Apply fresh grease. Finally, you can apply a fresh coat of grease to the moving parts, as shown in the bottom photo. Use light machine oil for the height-adjusting screw and block, and white lithium grease for the sliding parts. Reverse the disassembly process to reinstall the table, and adjust it as described on page 137.

Table Alignment

In addition to checking the individual tables for flatness or twist, it's critical to check to make sure that the infeed and outfeed tables are parallel to each other and that neither droops or sags. It's important that the outfeed table be aligned with the cutterhead. That is, the arc of the cutterhead must align with or be slightly above the plane of the outfeed table. You can check for this with a metal or wood straightedge, just as you would when adjusting the knives; see page 145. If the outfeed table is either too high or too low, the workpiece will either catch on the table or create snipe at the end of the cut, as illustrated in the drawing below.

Adjusting the outfeed table

Here's a quick way to check outfeed table alignment. Start by lowering the outfeed table slightly. Set the infeed table for a light cut, turn on the jointer, and cut into a scrap until its end extends about 1" onto the outfeed table, as shown in the middle photo. Then turn off the jointer and raise the outfeed table until it just touches the bottom of the freshly jointed portion, as shown in the bottom photo. Test the adjustment by turning on the jointer, and continue jointing, stopping a couple inches into the cut to make sure the outfeed table fully supports the workpiece.

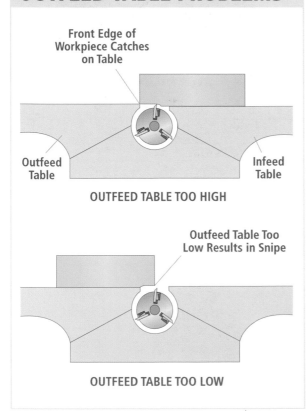

OUTFEED TABLE PROBLEMS

Front Edge of Workpiece Catches on Table

Outfeed Table

Infeed Table

OUTFEED TABLE TOO HIGH

Outfeed Table Too Low Results in Snipe

OUTFEED TABLE TOO LOW

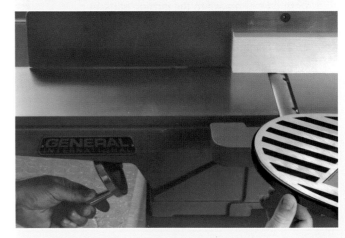

Checking table alignment

To check to see whether your tables are aligned, first raise the infeed table up to match the height of the outfeed table. Then lay a long, accurate straightedge along both tables and check to see whether they're level, as shown in the top photo. Quite often one of the tables will droop or sag.

Adjusting the tables

Most jointer manufacturers recommend adjusting the gibs (as shown in the middle photo) to bring the tables back into alignment; check your owner's manual for detailed gib-adjustment procedure. In most cases you'll tighten the gib screws differently. The screw nearest the cutterhead is tightened first, to apply sufficient pressure to counteract the weight of the table.

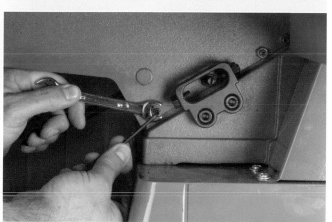

Shimming the tables

In some cases, adjusting the gibs won't remedy an out-of-alignment table. When this occurs, you'll need to insert shims between the table and the base to remove the sag or droop, as shown in the bottom photo. Brass and aluminum shim stock is available from most machinists' shops and some hardware stores and home centers. To prevent shims from twisting, it's important to always install them in pairs—one on each side of the table.

Removing Jointer Knives

To sharpen and grind jointer knives, you'll first need to remove them. Most manufacturers suggest that you remove only one knife at a time and replace this with a knife from a second set. If you don't have two sets of knives, consider purchasing some flat bar stock to insert while the knives are being sharpened. Removing all the knives at once can cause the cutterhead to warp.

Unplug the jointer

The first step in removing your jointer knives is to unplug the jointer, as shown in the top photo. To make sure it stays unplugged, it's a good idea to drape the cord over one of the tables as shown so it'll be in plain sight as you work.

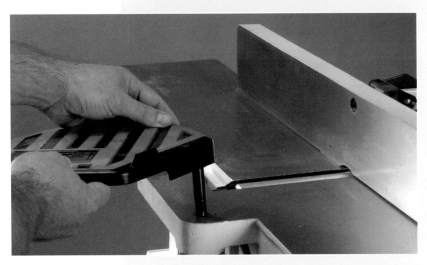

Lock or remove the guard

Next you'll want to remove the guard or lock it out of the way, as shown in the middle photo, to gain full access to the knives. Then rotate the cutterhead (use the drive belt for this) to expose one knife at a time, and mark each knife in turn and the cutterhead so that you can return the knives to their original slots.

Lock the cutterhead in place

Since you'll be loosening and tightening bolts in the gib slots of the cutterhead, you don't want the cutterhead moving about. Some jointers come with a built-in cutterhead lock. On jointers without a lock, just insert a scrap-wood wedge between the cutterhead and infeed or outfeed table to lock it in place, as shown in the bottom photo.

Remove the clamp bar and knife

Now you can use the recommended wrench to loosen the gib bolts (top inset photo) and lift out the clamp bar or gib. With the clamp bar removed, the next step is to carefully lift out the knife as shown in the top photo. **Safety note:** Even when dull, jointer knives are capable of making a nasty cut; use extra care when handling the knives. Note that on some jointers, you'll need to first remove the knife and then the clamp bar or gib.

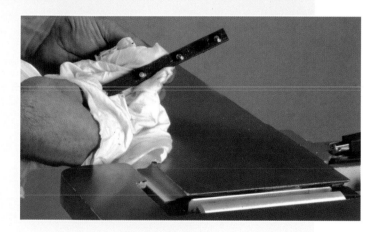

Clean the slot and clamp bar

Once the clamp bar and knife have been removed, take a moment to clean both of them with a soft rag, as shown in the middle photo, and check the clamp bar as described in the sidebar below. Then rub your fingertips gently over the surfaces and edges of the slot to check for burrs. If you find any, remove them with a non-abrasive pad or a smooth mill file.

PREVENTING KNIFE SHIFT

One of the main hassles of adjusting jointer knives—the knives shift as you tighten the gib bolts—is usually caused by burrs on the clamp bar or heads of the gib bolts. This can be greatly reduced and even prevented by filing the heads of the gib bolts and the faces of the clamp bars smooth with a mill file, as shown in the photo at right.

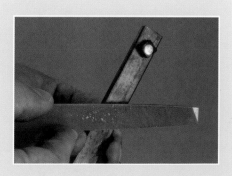

Grinding Jointer and Planer Knives

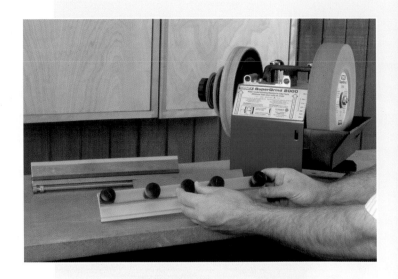

Because of their width, we recommend that you have your jointer and planer knives sharpened professionally. The only exception to this is if you have a wet-grinding system like the Tormek system shown here, with its jointer/planer knife-sharpening jig. This system is quite capable of handling most home-shop planer knives. The Tormek system is water-cooled grinding at its best—there's no chance of overheating and damaging the knife. Instructions on how to use the Tormek system are described below.

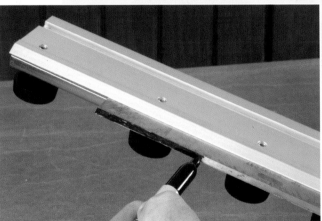

If you don't have a wet-grinding system and haven't used a local sharpening service in the past, check with your woodworking buddies or the local woodworking club or guild for a recommendation. We've had mixed results over the years from sharpening services. Although most do a fair job, occasionally you'll run up against one that doesn't. Check to make sure that they've sharpened jointer and planer knives before, and be careful to give exact instructions as to desired angle. We had one service grind our knives to the wrong angle because we assumed that they'd duplicate the existing angle. They didn't, and the knives had to be reground.

Clamp the knife in the holder
To sharpen a jointer or planer knife with the Tormek system, begin by inserting the knife in the holder as shown in the top photo, making sure that it rests against the stop along its entire length.

Color the bevel
Next, color the bevel along its length with a permanent marker so that you can see where the grinding occurs when setting the grind angle, as shown in the middle photo.

Position the holder

Now place the blade holder on the support as shown in the top left photo. Adjust the grinding length to match your blade. This is done by adjusting the stops, as shown in the top right photo, and ensures that the knife doesn't run off the edge of the stone during grinding.

Set the edge angle

To set the edge or grinding angle, start by roughly positioning the height of the jig with the holder height wheels. Then adjust the angle by turning the adjusting screw, as shown in the middle photo. What you want here is for the bevel to lie flat on the stone; just make sure that the holder does not touch the holder support. Then check the angle by turing the stone by hand; the stone should make marks on the bevel from the tip to the heel. Slide the knife back and forth to make sure it makes marks along the full length of the knife.

Set the grinding depth

Now you can set the grinding depth. This is done by raising the holder wheels, as shown in the bottom photo. Turn the wheels the same amount to ensure an even bevel. Unlock the locking screws for the holder posts, allowing the holder to lower the amount you have raised the wheels.

Start grinding

Fill up the water trough and then turn on the grinder. Slide the holder and knife with even pressure from side to side until the holder butts up against the end stops, as shown in the top photo. It's important to keep the holder and knife moving at all times.

Grind until the holder hits the rest

Continue grinding with even pressure until the holder hits the holder support along its entire length, as shown in the middle photo. Grinding is then complete, and you can move on to the next knife. For blades longer than 10", you'll have to slide the blade over in the holder and grind in two steps.

Hone the bevel

Grinding a knife will create a burr on its back. This can be quickly removed by honing. Just press the back of the knife against the leather honing wheel, as shown in the bottom photo. Once you've honed the back of the bevel, reverse the knife and hone the bevel. Repeat this procedure a couple of times to create a razor-sharp knife.

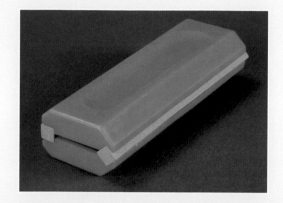

Honing Jointer Knives

The knives in your jointer will eventually dull and need to be resharpened. There are two basic ways you can handle this. If your knives are in reasonable shape (no nicks or severely blunted edges), it may be possible to hone them in place as described below. It's important to note that honing doesn't replace sharpening—it simply lengthens the time required between sharpenings.

Honing jig

There are a couple of honing jigs available for quickly bringing up a fresh edge on your jointer or planer knives. The one shown in the top photo has two different-shaped stones embedded in a plastic holder. When using one of these, make sure that the knives are clean and that the machine is unplugged prior to sharpening.

Hone the bevel

To use a honing jig, butt the stone of the jig up against the knife and push it forward in a long, gentle stroke, as shown in the middle photo. Make sure to keep the stone pressed firmly against the knife, or you'll alter the bevel angle. A couple of strokes per knife is all you'll need.

Hone the back

Then hone the back of the knife as shown in the bottom photo to remove any burr created by honing the bevel.

Adjusting Jointer Knives

Many woodworkers feel that some form of magic is required to adjust jointer knives accurately. Granted, this can be tricky—but all it really takes is patience. Much depends on what tools you use to adjust the knives. We'll describe the three most common methods here: stick, magnetic knife-holding jigs, and dial indicator.

THE STICK METHOD

Adjusting a jointer with a stick has been around for as long as jointers have been made—it's a simple technique but takes a lot of patience. The patience is required mainly because of the inherent movement that's caused when adjustments are tightened down. Typically, when a screw or bolt is fully tightened, it causes the part it's being tightened against to shift or twist. Even a slight movement can throw knife alignment off. And this is where the patience comes in (see the sidebar on page 139 for an excellent way to reduce this movement). Adjusting the knives on a jointer is very straightforward, but it does require a lot of back-and-forth adjusting—set the knives, check them, loosen and readjust, check them again, readjust...you get the idea.

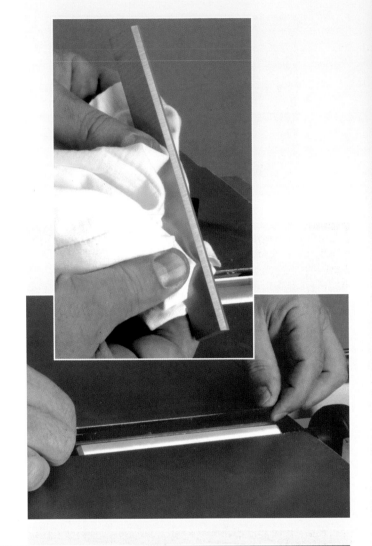

Clean and install the knives

To use the stick method for adjusting jointer knives, start by unplugging the machine. Since you'll likely be adjusting the knives because they've been sharpened, take the time to clean the slots and locking bars with mineral spirits. Then clean a knife (as shown in the top photo) and insert the knife and locking bar in the slot as shown in the middle photo. Tighten the nuts or screws so they're friction-tight—that is, they're held in place but can still be adjusted.

Position the fence

Next, slide the jointer fence to one side of the table, as shown in the bottom photo.

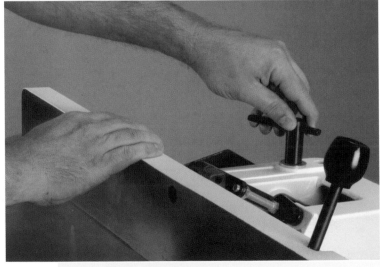

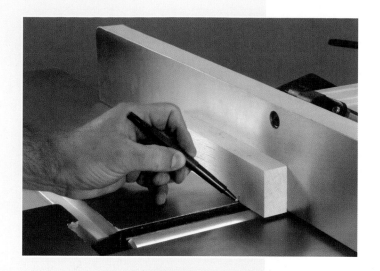

Mark the stick

Then select a scrap of straight wood that's about 8" to 10" long, and place the stick on the outfeed table so that it extends past the cutterhead and over the infeed table, as shown in the top photo. Make a mark on the stick where it touches the edge or beginning of the outfeed table.

Rotate the cutterhead

Now rotate the cutterhead toward the infeed table by hand (don't grab the cutterhead to do this; instead rotate it by moving the drive belt) so that it lifts the stick and drags it forward slightly, as shown in the middle photo. If the knife doesn't touch the stick, adjust it up so that it does. What you're looking for here is about $1/8$" of movement. This means the cutterhead is roughly 0.003" above the outfeed table. If it drags the stick more than that, it's too high and needs to be adjusted down.

Make a second stick mark

Once you've got the knife adjusted so that it lifts and drags the stick about $1/8$", make a second mark on the stick where it touches the beginning of the outfeed table, as shown in the bottom photo. These two marks then define the arc of the cutterhead at the desired height. If all the knives lift and drag the stick the same distance (on both ends), the knives are in perfect alignment. Sounds simple, huh?

Adjusting a knife

The knives in many jointers are positioned by way of a set of leveling screws. These screws thread into the cutterhead, and the knives rest on them. You can raise or lower each end of the knife separately by raising or lowering the screws. Alternatively, the knives may be held in place by the friction applied by the clamping bar or gib. In cases like this, it's easiest to set the knife a bit high and then tap it into alignment with a block of wood, as shown in the top photo.

Reset the fence and check alignment

After the knife is set on one side, slide the fence over to the other side of the table as shown in the middle photo. Then place the stick against the fence so that the first mark you made touches the beginning of the outfeed table. Rotate the cutterhead and check to see whether the stick is dragged the same length, as shown in the middle inset photo.

Readjust as necessary

Odds are that it won't drag the same length, and you'll need to adjust the knife. Use a scrap of wood to force the knife up or down and then recheck. Then tighten the locking bar and recheck with the stick. Adjust, tighten, and recheck. Repeat as many times as necessary by sliding the fence back and forth to both extremes of the table and checking until the stick is dragged the same amount on each side of each knife.
Repeat this procedure for each knife in the cutterhead.

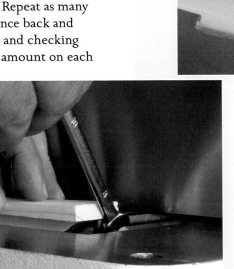

THE DIAL-INDICATOR METHOD

For the utmost in accuracy, you can use a dial indicator to adjust your jointer knives. Although a dial indicator takes a bit of time to set up, once set you can use it to accurately adjust your knives in thousandths of an inch.

Position cutterhead at top dead-center

To use a dial indicator to adjust your jointer knives, start by positioning the cutterhead so that a knife is at top dead-center, as described in the sidebar below. Once in place, secure the cutterhead by wedging a scrap between the cutterhead and the table, or by using the cutterhead lock as shown in the top photo.

Loosen a knife

Now you can loosen the gib or clamp-bar screws that secure the knife, as shown in the middle photo. Make sure to loosen these to friction-tight only. Alternatively, if you've installed freshly sharpened blades, take the time to clean the slots and locking bars with mineral spirits. Then clean a knife and insert the knife and locking bar in the slot before tightening the screws.

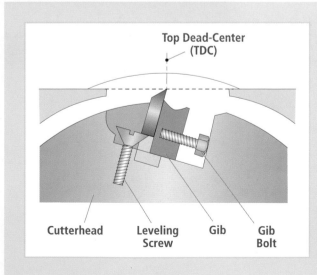

Top Dead-Center
(TDC)

Cutterhead Leveling Gib Gib
Screw Bolt

FINDING TOP DEAD-CENTER

Top dead-center is the top of an arc made by the cutterhead, as illustrated in the drawing at left. To locate top dead-center, place a flat scrap of wood on the outfeed table so it extends over the cutterhead. Rock the cutterhead back and forth until the cutting edge of the knife just barely touches the underside of the scrap, and make a mark on the fence.

Position the indicator

Next, position the dial indicator on the outfeed table so that its arm rests directly above the tip of the knife, as shown in the top photo. It's a good idea to clamp a square scrap to the outfeed table to keep the dial indicator at the same reference point along the table. Some indicators (like the one shown here) have a magnetic base that makes it easy to lock the unit firmly in place on the table.

Adjust the indicator

Adjust the position of the indicator's tip so that the knives will be set above the table the height recommended by the manufacturer; see your owner's manual for specifics. Most dial indicators have a fine-adjustment knob that makes this easy, as shown in the middle photo.

Check knife and adjust

With the tip of the indicator resting on the knife at top dead-center, adjust the position of the knife so that the indicator reads the desired setting, as shown in the bottom photo.

Reposition the indicator

Now slide the indicator to the opposite end of the table and position its tip over the top dead-center of the knife, as shown in the top photo. If you clamped a scrap to the outfeed table (as described earlier), this is as simple as sliding the indicator along the scrap wood.

Check the other end of the knife

Check the indicator and adjust the knife accordingly. Here again, how you adjust the knife will depend on your jointer. Some use leveling screws to raise or lower the knives; others are held in place via the clamping bar or gib. With this style you'll need to tap the knife in position with a scrap of wood before tightening the gib bolts, as shown in the middle photo.

Recheck the first end

Slide the indicator back to the other end and recheck as shown in the bottom photo. Repeat this sliding, checking, and adjusting until both ends of the knife read the same. Gently tighten each gib screw in turn and recheck, adjusting as necessary. Then tighten the gib screws or bolts, working from the center toward the ends. Rotate the cutterhead and repeat for each knife.

MAGNETIC KNIFE-HOLDING METHOD

There are a number of magnetic knife-setting jigs on the market that make adjusting knives less of a chore. They use a set of strong magnets to hold the knife in perfect position while you tighten the locking bolts.

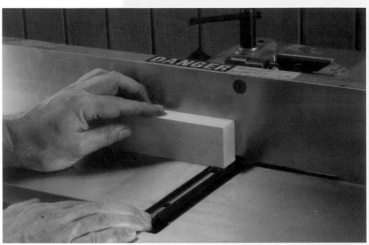

Locate top dead-center

To use one of these jigs, you'll need to find where the top of the cutterhead arc is, or top dead-center; see the sidebar on page 147. Locate top dead-center and make a mark on your fence, as shown in the top photo.

Scribe the fence

To save yourself the trouble of locating top dead-center every time you adjust the knives, use an awl to scribe or scratch a heavy line onto the fence, as shown in the middle photo. If necessary, darken the line with a felt-tip marker to help make it easier to see.

Position the jig

With top dead-center clearly marked on the fence, you can position the jig on the jointer. Align the marks on the jig with the line that you scribed in the fence, as shown in the bottom photo. With some jigs, the manufacturer suggests that you make an additional mark on the fence to correspond with a mark on the rear of the jig. This makes aligning the jig more precise.

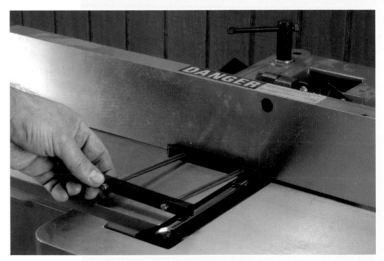

Loosen the gib bolts

To set the knives, lift the jig off the table and loosen the locking bar or gib bolts to just barely friction-tight, as shown in the top photo. Alternatively, you'll likely be adjusting the knives after they've been sharpened. Before you insert the sharpened knives, clean the cutterhead slots and the locking bars with mineral spirits, and wipe them off with a clean, dry cloth.

Adjust the knife

Reposition the magnetic-setting jig, taking care to align it with the marks that you made on the fence, as shown in the middle photo. As soon as the jig is in place, the magnets should pull the knife up into the perfect position. If they don't, carefully loosen the gib bolts a bit more until they do. If they extend too far (typically caused by overly strong gib springs, located under the knife), use a scrap (as shown here) to press the knife down until the magnets of the jig engage the table.

Lock down the knife

Once the knife is aligned by the jig, you can begin tightening the locking bar bolts or screws. Tightening sequence varies from one manufacturer to another—the most prevalent has you starting in the center and working out toward the ends. Tighten each bolt just a bit in turn, and continue tightening a little at a time until the locking bar is secure. If you tighten a bolt or screw completely, it can cause the knife to twist out of position. Run the jointer for a few minutes, and then retighten each bolt or screw. Rotate the cutterhead and repeat for the remaining knives.

Installing a Spiral Cutterhead

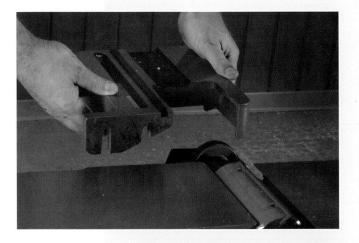

Cutterhead

Knife Insert

Insert Screw

Spiral cutterhead variations include spiral knives and spiral and helical cutterheads. With HSS spiral cutterheads, the knives wrap around the cutterhead in a spiral. The result is smoother cuts than with straight knives, especially when working on woods with highly figured grain. Spiral and helical cutterheads both use individual inserts as illustrated in the top drawing. Each insert is sharpened on all four edges and, when dull, can be rotated for a fresh edge. Also, if you nick the cutterhead, you can locate the nicked inserts and rotate them instead of removing, sharpening, and reinstalling all the knives. Installing a spiral cutterhead uses the same procedure you'd use to replace a straight cutterhead, as described below.

Remove fence arm and pulley

Start by unplugging your jointer. Then remove the guard, the fence, and the fence assembly bracket, as shown in the middle photo. Lower both the infeed and the outfeed table for better access to the cutterhead. Remove the pulley guard, and then disconnect the drive belt from the cutterhead by loosening the pulley setscrew and sliding the pulley off the end of the cutterhead, as shown in the bottom photo.

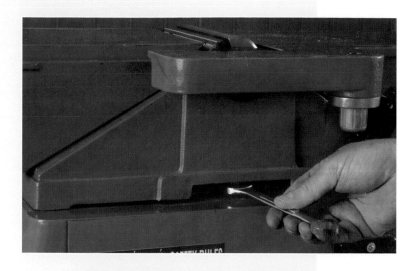

Loosen and remove cutterhead nuts

The cutterhead is typically secured to the base by way of blocks and bolts. Loosen and remove these as shown in the top photo. Check your owner's manual for specifics.

Lift out the old cutterhead

At this time you should be able to lift out the cutterhead, as shown in the middle photo. If the cutterhead doesn't pull out easily, you may need to rock it back and forth slightly while lifting—this usually does the trick.

Install the spiral cutterhead

Now you can install the spiral cutterhead by reversing the disassembly procedure, as shown in the bottom photo. Once in place, you'll need to adjust the outfeed table as described on page 136. Then adjust the infeed table for a light cut, turn on the jointer, and test the cut.

Planer Anatomy

A planer consists of a cutter-head supported by posts or a frame above a bed, as illustrated in the drawing at right. A motor, either universal or induction, drives the cutterhead via a belt. Belt- or chain-driven rollers push and pull a workpiece past the cutterhead. The cutterhead is typically raised or lowered by way of a threaded spindle. On larger planers, the cutterhead is fixed and the table or bed is raised and lowered—either manually or by way of a belt or a chain driven by a separate motor.

Depending on the size of the planer, it may also have a metal bar called a chip-breaker in front of the cutterhead, which breaks off chips lifted by the cutterhead and helps direct them out of the planer. Larger planers often also employ a pressure bar after the cutterhead to hold the stock firmly against the bed and prevent it from lifting up after the cut. Additional workpiece support is provided on many planers by extensions, whether stamped metal, cast iron, or rollers. Larger planers often have a pair of metal feed rollers set into the planer bed to help reduce friction.

EXPLODED VIEW

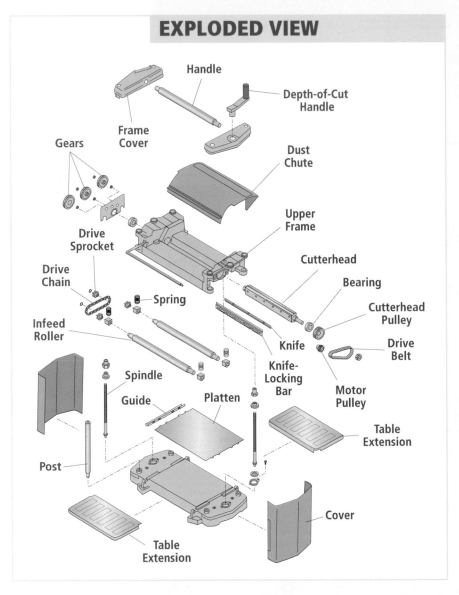

Handle

Depth-of-Cut Handle

Frame Cover

Gears

Dust Chute

Drive Sprocket

Upper Frame

Drive Chain

Cutterhead

Bearing

Spring

Cutterhead Pulley

Infeed Roller

Knife

Drive Belt

Spindle

Knife-Locking Bar

Guide

Platten

Motor Pulley

Post

Table Extension

Cover

Table Extension

Planer Cleaning/ Inspection

Regardless of their size, most planers get worked pretty hard. We've surfaced literally thousands of board feet with a small portable planer. The secret to its longevity? Regular maintenance. In many cases, all we're talking about is simply keeping the planer clean and inspecting it periodically.

Clean the posts

Besides the cutterhead and rollers, the posts of a planer are subject to the most movement because you're constantly changing the depth of cut. No matter whether your cutterhead or table moves, it's important to keep the posts as clean as possible. For the most part, all this takes is wiping them down regularly with a clean, dry cloth, as shown in the top left photo. If you've been planing resinous woods (like pine), it may be necessary to use mineral spirits or lacquer thinner to remove pitch and gum deposits.

Clean the bed and extensions

Sawdust and chips left in a planer will eventually affect its performance by gumming up gears and feed rollers and even forcing the cutterhead out of alignment. If you get in the habit of cleaning the bed and extensions (middle right photo) before you use the planer, you'll be pleased to find that not only will the planer last longer, but also it'll cut more precisely.

Clean the rollers

Even with good dust collection, sawdust and chips will still find a way to weasel their way into the drive gears of the planer. This is to be expected, since a planer is removing such copious amounts of wood. At least a couple times per year, and before and after a large planing job, it's a good idea to wipe down the infeed and outfeed rollers with a clean cloth, as shown in the bottom photo. Be careful here to stay away from the cutterhead, to prevent a nasty cut. After cleaning, inspect both the infeed and outfeed rollers to make sure nothing is embedded in them. Remove any chips you find with a pointed stick to keep from damaging the rollers.

Inspect the knives

Most planer manufacturers recommend that you regularly inspect the planer knives with a mirror for wear and tear (as shown in the top photos), as well as double-checking that the gib bolts are tight—typically every 50 hours of use; consult your owner's manual for recommended intervals. Regardless of the quality of the planer, planing is hard on the machine. There's a lot of inherent vibration, and the gib bolts can and do loosen over time. This is one of those preventive maintenance tasks that really can save you from having downtime and expensive repairs.

Bed flatness

Just as with the tables of a jointer, the bed of a planer must be flat and true in order to make accurate cuts. It's a good idea to periodically check the bed of your planer to make sure it's flat. To do this, place a known-accurate straightedge diagonally across the bed as shown in the middle photo. Then check for gaps with a feeler gauge. Any gaps over 0.010" should be repaired. Cast-iron beds can be reground and sheet-metal beds can be hammered flat at any reliable machine shop.

Bed twist

In addition to checking to make sure your planer bed is flat, you should also check it periodically for twist. The easiest way to do this is with a pair of shop-made "winding sticks," as shown in the bottom photo. Place the sticks on the bed about 1 to 2 inches in from each edge. Then sight along the sticks at a low angle to check for twist. If you detect a twist, the bed will need to be reground.

Planer Lubrication

The type, amount, and frequency of lubrication that your planer will require depends on the type of planer and how frequently and hard you use it.

Bed and extensions

Since the beds on most portable planers are sheet metal, we prefer to use a spray-on coating as shown in the top photo. We've found that these new coatings do a better job over time of protecting sheet metal than paste wax, and they create a really slick surface that reduces workpiece friction. Most of these are sprayed on and then buffed a few minutes later, once the coating dries.

For cast-iron beds and extensions, we prefer paste wax. After you've cleaned the bed and extensions (page 155), wipe on a light coat of wax as shown in the middle photo. After it has dried to a haze, buff the surface with a clean, dry cloth. It's also a good idea to wax the tables before and after a large project where the jointer gets a lot of use. As always, lubricate the bed and extensions periodically, and before and after big planing jobs.

Rollers

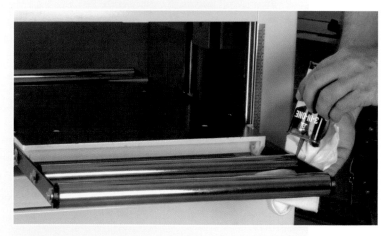

Metal rollers that are set into beds to reduce friction should be coated with paste wax as well. The bearings, if they're not sealed, may require lubrication as well. Sleeve bearings will benefit from a few drops of light machine oil (bottom photo). Feed rollers should not be lubricated, as they will lose their ability to grip lumber. If you have plastic or rubber feed rollers, you can apply platen rejuvenator—it's available at office machine repair stores, where it's used to rejuvenate rollers on typewriters, printers, and copiers. You just spray it on and then wipe it off. It'll refresh the surface, removing any slick or worn spots.

Posts

For the cutterhead or table to move smoothly up and down when adjusting the depth of cut, you'll need to keep the posts clean (page 155) and well lubricated. A drop or two of light machine oil on each post is all it takes, as shown in the top photo. To prevent sawdust from glomming onto the post and turning into a thick goo, wipe away any excess oil with a clean, dry cloth.

Gear trains

The gear system within a planer is primarily responsible for turning the infeed and outfeed rollers. Since these gears are in constant use, they will benefit from periodic lubrication. On smaller portable planers, the belts are often plastic and require no lubrication. Larger planers use chains and metal gears—sometimes sealed in an oil-filled gearbox, as illustrated in the bottom drawing. Consult your owner's manual for both the recommended lubricant and the suggested frequency of lubrication

(bottom photo). Depending on use, the frequency could vary anywhere from once a day to once or twice a year.

PLANER LUBRICATION POINTS

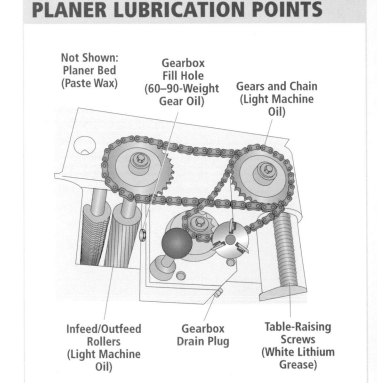

Not Shown: Planer Bed (Paste Wax)

Gearbox Fill Hole (60–90-Weight Gear Oil)

Gears and Chain (Light Machine Oil)

Infeed/Outfeed Rollers (Light Machine Oil)

Gearbox Drain Plug

Table-Raising Screws (White Lithium Grease)

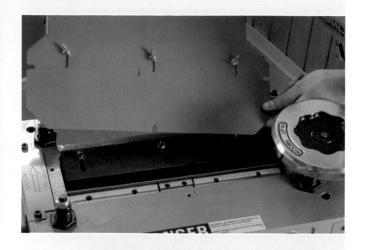

Adjusting Planer Knives

Because the cutterhead on a planer is suspended above the bed and not set between tables like on a jointer, the only accurate way to position and adjust the knives is to use a magnetic holding jig.

Remove the hood

The first step to using a magnetic knife-setting jig for the planer is to unplug the planer and remove the dust hood or chip deflector to gain access to the knives, as shown in the top photo. In many cases, the hood or deflector is held on with a pair of thumbscrews. **Safety note:** The exposed knives are very sharp; exercise extreme caution when working around these. It's also a good idea to clear away any dust or chips with a blast of compressed air or with a vacuum.

Loosen the gib bolts

Once you've gained access to the knives, the next step is to loosen the gib screws or bolts that press the gib into the knives to hold them in place in the cutterhead, as shown in the middle photo. Note: If your planer uses elevating screws to adjust the height of the knives, back these off so that they don't interfere with the operation of the magnetic jig; consult your owner's manual for more on this.

REMOVING PLANER KNIVES

Loosen the gib bolts and insert the tip of a screwdriver under one of the gib screws or bolts and pry the gib up—it should come up easily, and if it doesn't, double-check to make sure that all the bolts are sufficiently loose. Once the gib is out, carefully lift out the knife. With the gib and knife removed from the cutterhead, take the time to clean out the slot. Remove any sawdust or chips with compressed air or a vacuum, and follow this with a clean, dry cloth. If you notice any pitch or resin deposits, dampen the cloth with some lacquer thinner or mineral spirits and scrub the slot clean. Clean the gib and knife as well before reinstalling them.

Back off the chip deflector

To better access the cutterhead, loosen the screws holding the chip deflector in place and slide it as far away from the cutterhead as possible, as shown in the top photo.

Position the knife

Some tool makers include a knife-setting guide with their planer, like the one shown in the middle drawing. A nice thought, but we find these a challenge to use, as you really need three hands: one to hold the guide, one to loosen and tighten gib screws, and one to raise or lower the knife. Magnetic setting jigs (like the ones shown in the bottom photo) for the planer work on the same principle as those for the jointer. A set of strong magnets are held in a plastic or metal head that fits the curve of the cutterhead. A third magnet in the jig holds the knife in position while you tighten the gib screws or bolts. Correct placement is achieved by butting one leg of the jig up against the edge of the cutterhead. Position a magnetic jig at each end of the cutterhead, following the manufacturer's directions. Press down on the jig so the magnets grip the cutterhead and the knife.

Lock the knife in place

Once you've got the knife in the correct position, go ahead and tighten the gib screws or bolts. Tighten these in small increments, working from the center of the knife to the edges until the knife is held securely in place, as shown in the bottom photo. Rotate the cutterhead and repeat this procedure for the remaining knives.

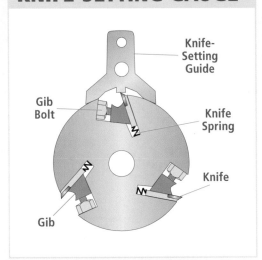

KNIFE-SETTING GAUGE

Knife-Setting Guide

Gib Bolt

Knife Spring

Knife

Gib

PORTABLE PLANER KNIVES

Changing knives on a portable planer can be more challenging than on a stationary planer, primarily because everything is shoehorned into a smaller package. The big issue is lack of knuckle room. The knife-changing

procedure, however, is similar to that of a stationary planer; the big difference is how the knives are held in place (see below).

Access the cutterhead. Accessing the cutterhead is simpler on most portable planers than it is for a stationary one. In general, all you have to do is remove the dust chute that covers the knives, as shown in the top photo, and there they are.

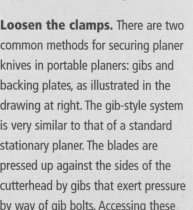

Loosen the clamps. There are two common methods for securing planer knives in portable planers: gibs and backing plates, as illustrated in the drawing at right. The gib-style system is very similar to that of a standard stationary planer. The blades are pressed up against the sides of the cutterhead by gibs that exert pressure by way of gib bolts. Accessing these bolts inside the slot in the cutterhead in a cramped space can be difficult. The other style—backing plates—is much more accessible. Here the knife is clamped between a backing plate and the cutterhead. Not only are the bolts easier to loosen, but also the knives are easier to get to.

Position the magnetic setting jig. As with a stationary planer, you'll find the easiest way to position portable planer knives is with a magnetic setting jig. The standard size of these is too large for the smaller cutterheads of portable planers, so the manufacturer makes a "mini" version where the magnets are held in a plastic body. Alternatively, some manufacturers include a set of custom jigs for their planers, as shown in the bottom photo.

KNIFE-CLAMPING OPTIONS

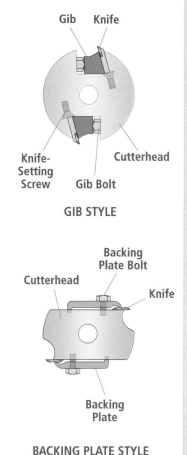

GIB STYLE

BACKING PLATE STYLE

Rapid-Change Planer Knives

Many of the newer portable planers feature double-sided blades that are quick and easy to change. For the most part, they use the backing plate–style knife clamping system described on page 161.

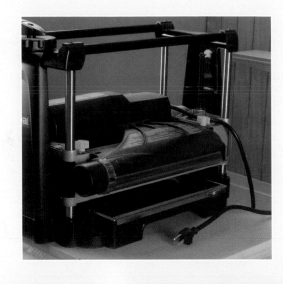

Unplug the planer

To change a set of rapid-change planer knives, begin by unplugging the planer and draping the cord over one of the extension tables as shown in the top photo.

Access the cutterhead

Next, lower the cutterhead as far down as it will go, as shown in the middle left photo. Then loosen and remove the screws that secure the dust chute to the planer and remove the dust chute as shown in the middle right photo. Rotate the cutterhead until it locks in place—on the Ryobi planer shown here, the cutterhead locks in place every 180 degrees once the dust chute has been removed. Replacing the chute disables the cutterhead lock. Make sure to move the cutterhead via the drive belt or threaded spindle— never by touching the cutterhead itself.

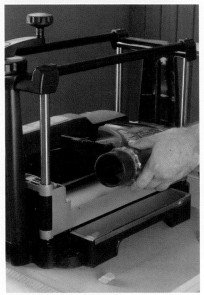

Loosen the knife-locking screws

Now you can loosen and remove the knife-locking screws or bolts, as shown in the bottom photo, and set them aside.

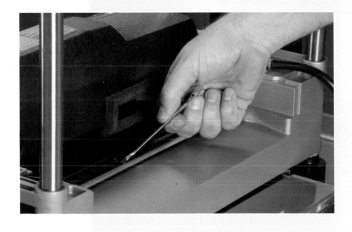

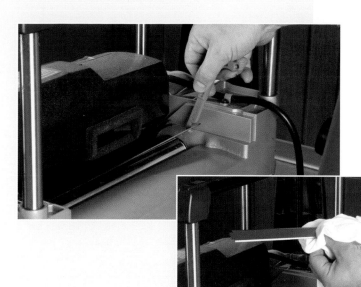

Remove and clean the knife

Most portable planers have tabs or recesses machined into the cutterhead to make it easier to remove the knives. Reach in carefully with your fingers and pull out the knife. The Ryobi planer comes with a plastic tool with a hook on one end and a magnet on the other that makes it easy to pull out a knife, as shown in the top photo. Then clean the blade with a soft cloth and apply a few drops of light machine oil; wipe the knife dry with the cloth as shown in the top inset photo.

Insert the knife

On a double-sided knife, the knife can then be flipped end for end to expose a fresh edge (or replaced if both sides are dull) and inserted into the cutterhead. On the Ryobi knives shown here, alignment is a snap, as tabs are machined into the knife as well as the locking bar. By engaging the respective tabs, alignment is assured. Other planers often use a lip machined into the locking bar to align a knife.

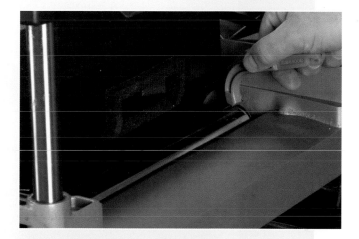

Tighten knife-lock screws

All that's left is to tighten the knife-lock screws as shown in the bottom photo. Here again, it's best to start in the middle of the cutterhead and work your way to each end, alternately tightening screws. Disengage the cutterhead lock, rotate the cutterhead, and repeat for the remaining knife. Replace the dust chute, plug in the planer, and test.

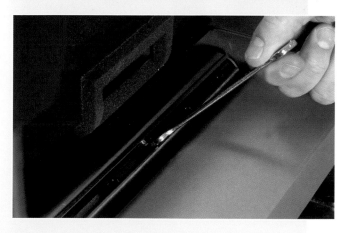

Adjusting Feed Rollers

On some planers, particularly planer/molders, you can adjust the feed-roller pressure to compensate for different operations (like planing versus molding) and types of wood. Typical clearances for larger planers are illustrated in the top drawing.

Loosen locknut

To adjust the feed rollers, start by loosening the jam nuts that lock the rollers in position, as shown in the middle photo. Note that located on these same posts are the nuts that control the spring pressure—these are factory-set and should not be fiddled with.

Insert the gauge block

Next, make a reference gauge block following the manufacturer's instructions in the owner's manual, or use the machined gauge block supplied or purchased from the manufacturer. Slide this gauge block under the center of the feed roller as shown in the bottom photo.

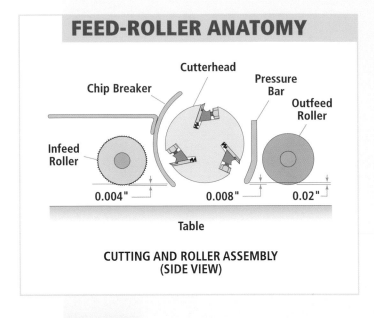

FEED-ROLLER ANATOMY

Cutterhead

Chip Breaker

Pressure Bar

Outfeed Roller

Infeed Roller

0.004" 0.008" 0.02"

Table

**CUTTING AND ROLLER ASSEMBLY
(SIDE VIEW)**

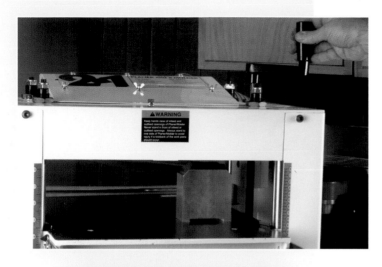

Adjust the feed rollers

Now raise the table (or lower the cutter-head) until the roller just barely touches the block, as shown in the top photo. Note that you should be able to slide the gauge block back and forth along the full width of the feed roller. In some cases, you may have multiple gauge blocks of varying heights designed for specific operations; make sure that you're using the correct block.

Check the clearance

Once the gauge block is in place, adjust the feed rollers by turning the threaded bushings on the posts as shown in the middle photo. Then slide the gauge block under the feed roller to its opposite end. Here again, it'll be adjusted correctly when you can just barely slide the guide block back and forth along the entire length of the feed roller.

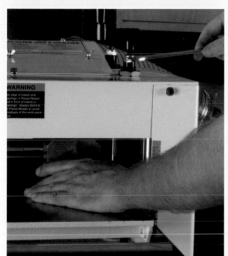

Adjust and tighten the locknuts

Adjust the feed rollers by rotating the adjustment nut as shown in the bottom photo. Then retighten the locknuts and recheck for clearance under the feed roller along its entire length; repeat this procedure for the outfeed roller, if desired.

Adjusting the Cutterhead

Outside of adjusting the knives and feed rollers on a portable planer (pages 144–151 and pages 164–165, respectively), there's not a lot more you can do in terms of adjustment. That's because most portable planers don't have an adjustable pressure bar or chip breaker, as illustrated in the drawing at right. It's not that you can't adjust them; they're not there at all. You'll usually only find these on larger planers with knives 15" and wider.

On portable planers, there is nothing directly on each side of the cutterhead. Instead, these smaller planers rely on the infeed and outfeed rollers instead of a pressure bar, and they depend on sharp blades to prevent chip-out.

On larger planers, not only can you adjust the pressure bar and chip breaker (see your owner's manual for more on these adjustments), but you should also adjust the cutterhead so that it's parallel to the planer's bed; see the opposite page.

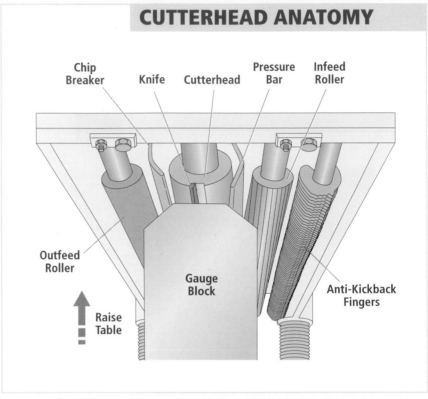

CUTTERHEAD ANATOMY

Chip Breaker · Knife · Cutterhead · Pressure Bar · Infeed Roller · Outfeed Roller · Gauge Block · Raise Table · Anti-Kickback Fingers

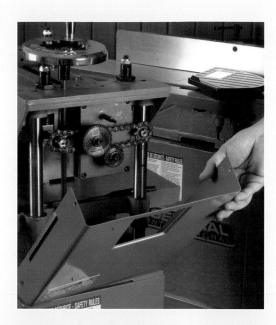

Access the cutterhead

Consult your owner's manual for the recommended procedure for checking and adjusting the cutter-head/bed parallelism. In most cases, the manufacturer suggests that you remove one or both of the side panels of the planer for better access, as shown in the top photo.

Position the gauge block

Next, insert a wood gauge block made out of a scrap of hardwood, or a machined gauge block supplied by the manufacturer, under the center of the cutterhead so it just touches one of the knives, as illustrated in the drawing on page 166 and shown in the middle photo. Here's one instance where a wood gauge block may be better than a machined metal one—since you're contacting the knife with the block, a wood block can't damage the knife.

Adjust for parallel

Typically, there is a set of bevel gears that will allow adjustment of the position of the cutterhead or table. Loosen the jam nut and adjust the bevel gear until you can slide the gauge block back and forth under the cutterhead, as shown in the bottom photo (this is a top view looking down into the cutterhead; the gauge block is below the cutterhead). Then you can retighten the jam nut and check the clearance again with the gauge block.

Electrical Repairs

The electrical system on most jointers and planers is simple and straightforward. Power enters through the plug and continues up the electrical cord. On its way to the motor, it passes through the on/off switch, which serves to control the flow of electricity.

Switch replacement

To replace a switch, remove the cover plate and gently pull out the switch. Then note the wire colors and locations before removing the old switch. The most reliable way to replace any power switch is to disconnect one wire at a time and connect it to the corresponding terminal on the replacement switch, as shown in the top photo.

Cord replacement

On some jointers and planers, you have to crawl under the machine to access the power connections. Other manufacturers offer detachable housings that provide relatively easy access. In any case, once the ends of the cord are in sight, make a note of wire colors, locations, and routing. Replace the cord by removing one wire at a time and installing the matching wire of the new cord, as shown in the middle photo. This way there won't be any wiring mistakes.

Replacing brushes

The universal motors on portable planers use brushes that will wear out over time. A spring inserted between an end cap/wire assembly and the brush pushes the brush against the armature. If the springs don't exert enough pressure, the brushes will make intermittent contact and your planer will operate sluggishly. Most manufacturers make changing brushes easy by providing accessible brush caps, like those shown in the bottom photo.

Just unscrew the cap and set it aside. If the springs are in good shape, they'll force out the metal end of the brush. If the springs are bad, you may need to pry out the metal end in order to pull out the brush. If the ends of the brushes are scarred, replace them. As to length, the general rule is if you've got less than $1/4$" of brush left, replace the brushes.

Portable Power Planers

For the most part, portable power planers are as rugged and dependable as their other portable power-tool cousins. The big difference here, though, is that when the cutting knives of the tool become dull, there's more work involved. Unlike saw blades and drill bits that can be changed in seconds, a power planer requires more time and attention. That's because cutterhead alignment is as critical here as it is with a jointer or planer. Knife-changing routines run from amazingly simple to downright difficult. If possible, ask a tool vendor to show you how the knives are changed.

Disposable knives

One of our favorite improvements to portable planers in recent years has been the introduction of disposable knives like those shown in the top photo. These double-sided knives can be discarded when both edges dull. Since they're both thinner and narrower than standard knives, they're less expensive. Add to this the fact that you don't have to wait a week or two for your knives to get sharpened, and they make a lot of sense.

Changing knives

To change a knife, first unplug the planer or remove its battery if it's cordless. Most knives are held in place with brackets. After you've removed the bolts, lift off the bracket and slide out the planer knife as shown in the middle photo. The Bosch planer shown here uses a unique knife retainer that virtually guarantees proper placement when the knives are reinstalled. The edge of the retainer that's opposite the cutting edge has a lip that fits in a groove in the cutterhead; as long as the knife is aligned on the retainer, repositioning the knife is amazingly easy. When the new knife is in place, tighten the retainer screws as shown in the bottom photo. Depending on the manufacturer of your planer, it may or may not come with some sort of knife-alignment gauge. Some planers come with a simple gauge that automatically aligns the planer knife in its retainer. Just position the knife with the retainer on the gauge, push the knife forward so it contacts the lip of the gauge, and tighten the retainer screws as shown.

■ TROUBLESHOOTING

As we've mentioned previously, the jointer and planer are real workhorses in the shop. Once aligned, they tend to run fairly trouble-free. When problems do arise, though, most are easily diagnosed and repaired.

JOINTER PROBLEMS AND SOLUTIONS

Jointer problems tend to be caused by either the knives or misaligned tables.

Rough cuts

Rough cuts on the jointer (as in the photo above) are most often caused by either dull knives or jointing in the wrong direction. Dull knives can't cleanly sever wood fibers, and the result is chip-out. The solution is to remove your knives (pages 138–139), sharpen them (pages 140–143) or have them sharpened, and install and adjust them (pages 144–151). Jointing against the grain (as described on page 54) will almost always result in a rough cut, as the wood fibers are unsupported and the knives will lift up and tear out chucks of wood instead of cleanly slicing through them.

Concave/convex cuts

Frequently you won't notice that a jointer is creating concave or convex cuts until you edge-joint a long board. The longer the board, the easier it is to detect. Both concave and convex cuts are caused by misaligned tables, as illustrated in the drawing at right. Concave cuts occur if either the outfeed table is too high or both tables are too high and not parallel. Edges that come out convex are caused by infeed and outfeed tables that are too low and not parallel.

CONCAVE/CONVEX CURVES

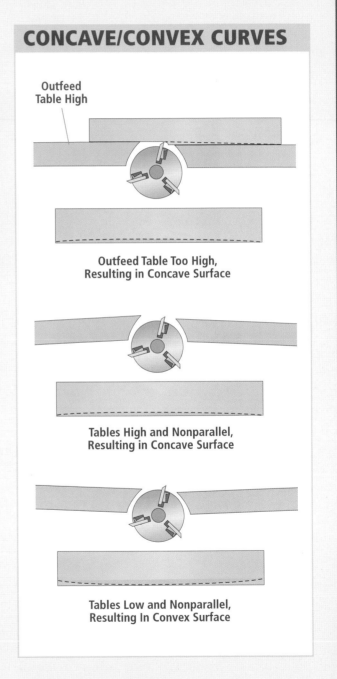

Outfeed Table High

Outfeed Table Too High, Resulting in Concave Surface

Tables High and Nonparallel, Resulting in Concave Surface

Tables Low and Nonparallel, Resulting In Convex Surface

Ripples

Ripples (like those shown in the top photo) are typically caused by using too fast of a feed rate. By pushing the workpiece over the knives too fast, the arced or scalloping cut that the knives makes is exaggerated that same way it does on a planer, as described on page 173. The solution? Slow down. Just make sure you don't go too slow, or friction can build up, resulting in burning.

Ribbed cut

A ribbed cut like the one shown in the photo above is most often caused by nicked knives. A recent workpiece had a metal fastener embedded in it, and when it hit the knives, it broke away a portion on the knives. Obviously, you'll eventually want to have all of your knives reground. But a quick fix is to loosen just one of the knives and slide it to one side. This will offset the nick, and your ribbed cut will disappear. Alternatively, if you are using a spiral cutterhead with individual inserts, simply locate the nicked inserts and rotate them to present a fresh edge.

Snipe on outfeed

Snipe on the outfeed end of a workpiece is the result of the outfeed table being too low or the cutterhead (the knives, actually) being too high, as illustrated in the drawing at left. The solution is to either adjust the outfeed table (see pages 136–137) or adjust the knives (pages 144–151).

SNIPE ON OUTFEED

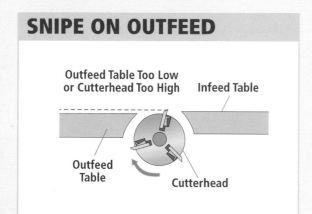

Outfeed Table Too Low or Cutterhead Too High   Infeed Table

Outfeed Table

Cutterhead

PLANER PROBLEMS AND SOLUTIONS

Common problems encountered on a planer are snipe, ribbed cuts, and rough cuts.

Snipe

When a thickness-planer cuts or dishes the ends of a board thinner than the middle portion of a board, the result is snipe (as shown in the photo above). If your knives are dull, they tend to lift the ends of the board as it enters the planer—so keep them sharp. The pressure rollers and table rollers are often the culprit. As a board enters or exits a planer, it's only in contact with one of the rollers. And the pressure of the roller often cocks the board up slightly into the cutterhead, resulting in a deeper cut. Common solutions include lifting the board up at the end of the cut, using an auxiliary table to prevent table rollers from cocking the board (page 68), and using the cutterhead lock feature (if your planer has one).

Ribbed cuts

The same thing that causes a ribbed cut on a jointer causes a ribbed cut on a planer—your knives are nicked. A workpiece with a metal fastener embedded in it struck the knives and broke away a portion, resulting in a ribbed cut, as shown in the top right photo on page 171. You'll eventually want to have all of your knives reground. But a quick fix is to loosen just one of the knives and slide it to one side. This will offset the nick, and your ribbed cut will disappear.

Alternatively, if you are using a spiral cutterhead with individual inserts, locate the nicked inserts and rotate or replace them to present a fresh edge.

Rough cuts

In most cases, a rough cut on a planer (top right photo) is caused by one of two things: You're feeding the workpiece into the planer wrong, or the knives are dull. Make sure to follow the general rule for grain direction when planing (page 64) and keep your knives sharp and adjusted properly (pages 159–163). You can also encounter a rough cut when planing wood with highly figured or squirrelly grain. Try feeding the wood into the planer at an angle, as described on page 64, to produce more of a shearing cut.

HOW RIPPLES ARE CREATED

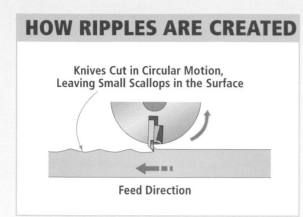

Knives Cut in Circular Motion,
Leaving Small Scallops in the Surface

Feed Direction

Ripples

A workpiece surface that is rippled is usually an indication that your feed rate is too fast. A fast feed rate will exaggerate the arced or scalloped cut that a round cutterhead makes, as illustrated in the drawing above and shown in the bottom photo on page 172.. Slowing down the feed rate will help reduce this, but by its very nature a planer will always produce some rippling.

Motor bogs down

When a planer bogs down, the motor is telling you that you're trying to take off more wood than it can handle. It could be too heavy of a cut, or it could be a moderate cut but on a very wide piece. The solution is simply to back off on the cut. Likewise, cutting into dense or abrasive woods

(like teak) can slow a motor down. On these woods you have to take multiple lighter passes. Finally, the motor could be telling you that your knives are dull and need sharpening, or it's just too small to handle the amount of wood that you're trying to remove.

Burning

Burning (like that shown in the photo above) occurs less frequently with a planer than it does on the jointer. That's because the most common cause of burning—too slow a feed rate—is less likely because the feed rate is set on a planer via the feed rollers. However, if the feed rollers slip and the workpiece doesn't move, friction will build up and burning will occur. To prevent burning, keep your feed rollers clean and adjusted properly (pages 164–165) and your bed table lubricated (page 157) to prevent a workpiece from catching. Taking light cuts instead of heavy cuts also helps reduce the likelihood of burning.

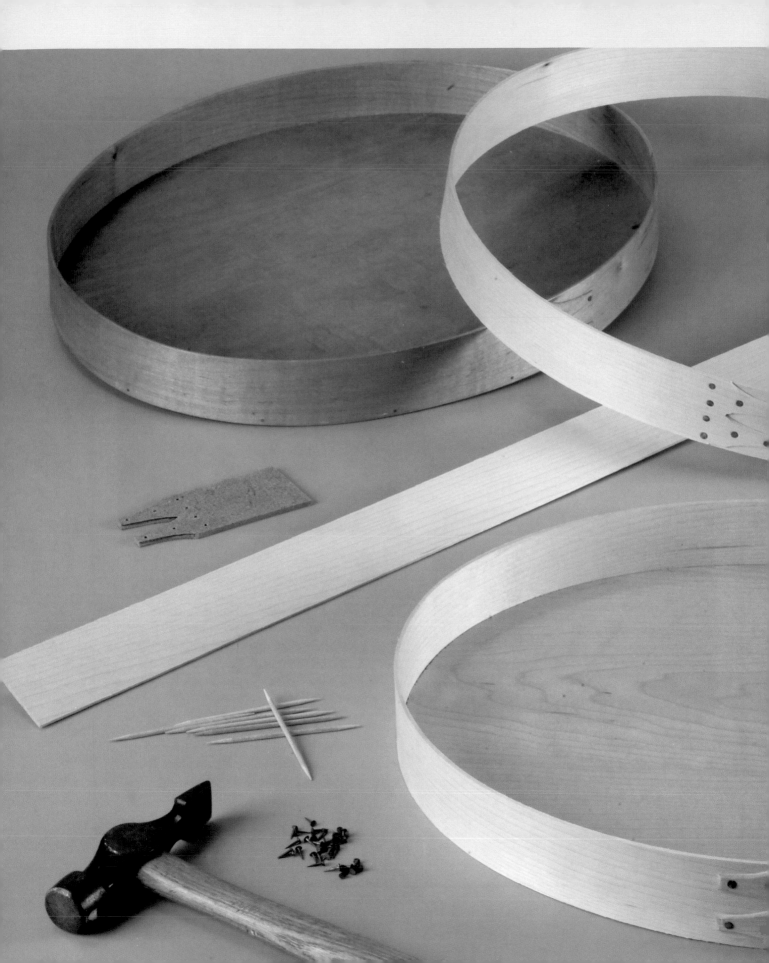

7 Jointer and Planer Projects

Odds are that you'll use a jointer and/or planer on virtually every project that you build. So when it came time to pick the projects for this book, we focused on projects where the jointer or planer played a major role in the construction. The first project in the chapter—a Shaker tray—relies on the planer to produce stock so thin it can be easily bent without the need for steam. The other two projects in this chapter—a hall mirror and a plant stand—both sport tapers that are best cut on the jointer. And each employs a different technique to cut the tapers.

Unassembled, the projects in this chapter look like scraps you'd find in your junk bin. But put the parts together, and you end up with three classic projects that will grace any interior: a Shaker tray, a hall mirror, and a plant stand.

Shaker Tray

Shaker trays, baskets, and boxes have been a favorite project of woodworkers for years. Their graceful curves and stately simplicity allow them to fit into almost any décor—from colonial to modern. Normally the thin wood sides of these pieces are steam-bent around a form and allowed to dry before the ends are secured to form an oval. The Shaker tray shown here, though, doesn't require this, as the oval is large and the curves are gradual. Even so, it's important that you select an appropriate wood for the project and cut it so the grain is oriented correctly; see below. Our Shaker tray consists of two parts: a band and a bottom; see the Exploded View on the opposite page. The ends of the band are secured with small copper tacks, and the band is attached to the bottom with "mini" dowels—round wood toothpicks. The copper tacks can be ordered from the folks at www.shakerovalbox.com.

Because you'll be planning the stock so thin, odds are that the planer will occasionally snap a band—that's why we suggest cutting at least three to begin with. Take your time here, and take light passes to minimize breakage. A dial caliper (page 49) makes checking the thickness a snap.

Rough-cut the band

Historically, the best woods for making bands have been tight-grained woods like hard maple, birch, and cherry. (We used birch for the tray shown here.) To make a band, start by ripping a 4-foot-long board into $1^1/2$"-wide strips. Then rip these into bands about $^3/16$" thick, as shown in the middle photo (a $^3/4$"-thick strip should yield three bands). Grain orientation is critical here—what you're looking for is quarter-sawn or rift-sawn grain (where the grain runs as close to perpendicular to the face of the band as possible) along the full length of the strip. If your band has plain-sawn grain, the band will break as it's bent.

Thickness-plane the band

Now you can thickness-plane the bands to a finished thickness of $^5/64$", as shown in the bottom photo. You'll need a planer sled or thin-stock sled for this as described on pages 94–95 and 108–109, respectively.

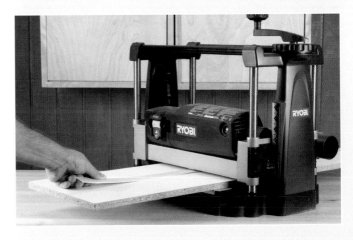

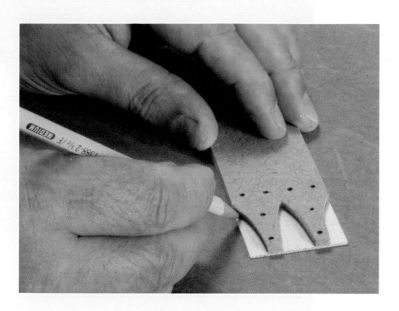

Lay out fingers and tack holes

The next step is to lay out the distinctive finger pattern on one end of the band. Use the pattern shown on page 178 for this. We suggest making a template from a piece of $1/8$" hardboard from this pattern, since odds are that you'll want to make more than one tray. Position the template on one end of the band and mark the fingers and the holes for the copper tacks that secure the ends of the band together as shown in the top photo.

EXPLODED VIEW

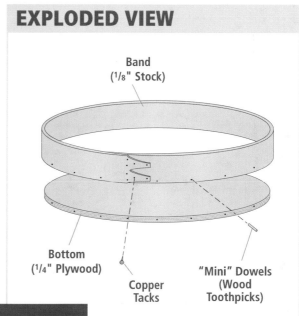

Band ($1/8$" Stock)

Bottom ($1/4$" Plywood)

Copper Tacks

"Mini" Dowels (Wood Toothpicks)

MATERIALS LIST

Part	Quantity	Dimensions
Band	1	$1\frac{1}{2}$" × 44" − $5/64$"
Bottom	1	$11\frac{1}{2}$" × 14" − $1/4$" plywood*
Tacks	8	copper, #2
Dowels	16	round wood toothpicks

* Sand to fit.

Cut the fingers

With the fingers laid out, you can cut them to shape. Although you can use a saw for this (band, saber, or coping), we've always found that it's easiest to cut the fingers out with a sharp utility knife. Take a series of light cuts until you've cut through the thin material, as shown in the top photo. Using a utility knife produces a cleaner edge than using a saw blade.

Bevel the ends of the fingers

Although it's not technically necessary, the ends of the fingers are beveled to create a smoother transition when they overlap the opposite end of the band. Here again, a utility knife with a sharp blade will make quick work of this, as shown in the middle photo. Hold the blade at roughly a 45-degree angle, and trim the perimeter edges of the fingers. As you near the intersection of two fingers, taper off on the angle to create a smooth transition.

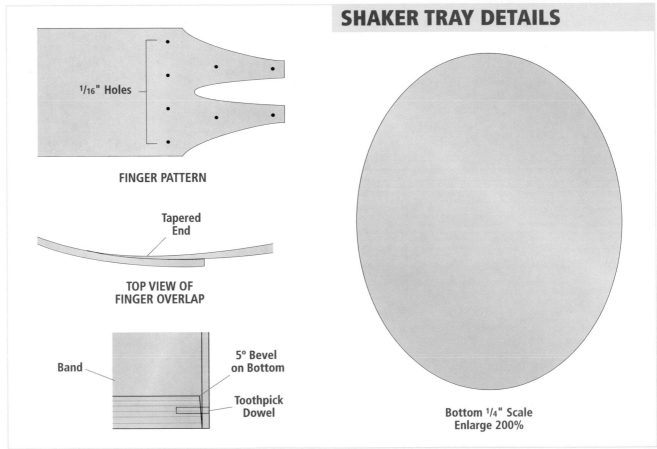

1/16" Holes

FINGER PATTERN

Tapered End

TOP VIEW OF FINGER OVERLAP

Band

5° Bevel on Bottom

Toothpick Dowel

SHAKER TRAY DETAILS

Bottom 1/4" Scale
Enlarge 200%

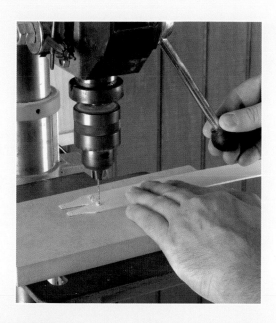

Drill the tack holes

Now you can drill the holes in the end of the band for the small copper tacks, as shown in the top photo. Because these holes are so small ($^1/_{16}$"), it's a good idea to centerpunch them lightly first to prevent the drill bit from wandering or bending off course.

Feather the end of the band

Since the ends of the band overlap where they're joined together, you need to feather the end of the band opposite the fingers so that you don't end up with a double thickness at the joint (see the detail drawing on page 178). The easiest way we've found to do this is on a belt/disk sander, as shown in the middle photo. Use a block of wood to hold the band flat on the sanding belt, and sand the end to a point and taper it back about 2" to 3". Alternatively, you can plane a taper with a small block plane or sand it by hand.

Rough-cut the bottom

The bottom is just a piece of $^1/_4$" plywood that matches the wood of the band. Enlarge the bottom pattern on page 178 to 200 percent and transfer this to your plywood. Then cut the plywood to the rough bottom shape, taking care to stay on the waste side of the pattern line. We used a band saw for this (bottom photo), but you can cut out the bottom with a scroll saw, saber saw, or coping saw.

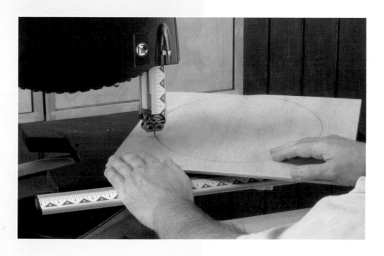

Wrap band around bottom and mark

Now for the fun part—bending the band. Start by positioning the tapered end of the band around the midpoint of the long side of the oval plywood bottom. Then carefully—and gently—wrap the band all the way around the bottom, taking care to support both fingers as you near the end. (If you don't support the fingers, they'll split.) Holding the band in place with one hand, scoot the fingers over $1/4$" to $1/2$", to make a slightly smaller band (to allow for sanding the bottom later), and then use a pencil to mark where the ends of the fingers overlap the band, as shown in the top photo. Then release the band from the bottom.

Secure the band with tacks

With the band marked, now you can secure the ends with copper tacks. We clamped a piece of black pipe to our bench as an anvil (middle photo). Bend the band so the fingers align with the marks you made previously (here again, be sure to support the fingers). Position the holes directly over the center of the pipe anvil, and drive tacks through the holes in the band. As a tack passes through both ends of the band and strikes the anvil, the end of the tack will deflect to the side and pinch the ends of the band together; repeat for all the holes, repositioning the band on the anvil as you go to make sure each hole is centered directly over the anvil.

Bevel-sand the bottom

With the band complete, you can finish up the bottom. To get a tight fit, sand the perimeter of the bottom at about a 5-degree bevel, as shown in the detail drawing on page 178. Using a disk sander with a tilting table is the easiest way to do this (as shown in the bottom photo), but you can tilt the table on a drill press for a drum sander, or do it by hand. Sand up to the pattern line as you work around the perimeter.

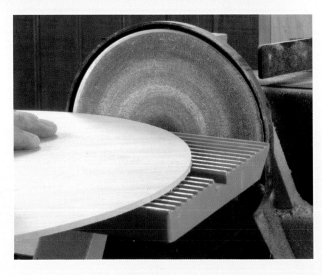

Test the fit

Once you've sanded the bottom, test to see how it fits in the band, as shown in the top photo. You're looking for a snug fit that doesn't require a lot of pressure to fit the parts together. If the fit is too snug, sand the bottom until it fits.

Drill holes for the toothpicks

With the band and the bottom happily mated together, the final step is to secure the two parts together with mini dowels (round wood toothpicks). To do this you'll first need to drill a series of holes around the perimeter of the tray, centered on the thickness of the plywood, as shown in the middle photo. Stay away from the tight-radius ends of the tray, as drilling here often leads to splitting. The holes are $1/16$" diameter and only $1/4$" to $3/8$" deep.

Insert toothpicks and sand flush

Apply a tiny dollop of glue to the end of a toothpick and insert it in a hole, as shown in the bottom photo. Repeat for the remaining holes. Snip the toothpicks as close to the surface of the band as possible, using a pair of diagonal pliers or scissors. Then sand the ends flush with a piece of sandpaper wrapped around a block of wood (bottom inset photo). Sand the entire tray and apply the finish of your choice.

Hall Mirror

It's surprising sometimes what you can do with just five pieces of wood. The elegant Craftsman-inspired hall mirror shown here is an excellent example of this. It consists of a pair of tapered stiles, a top and bottom rail, and a molding strip; see the Exploded View on the opposite page. Although we fitted the frame with a mirror and a set of hooks, you could leave out the hooks or even use it as a picture frame. Most Craftsman-style projects were originally made of quartersawn white oak, but we used quartersawn red oak, as it's more readily available.

Cut the half-laps

The four main parts of the frame (stiles and rails) are joined together with half-laps. The half-laps on the top rail are angled to match the taper of the stiles and are cut later. Start by cutting the parts to size per the materials list on the opposite page. Then cut the half-laps in the bottom rail and the top and bottom of the stiles, as shown in the middle photo and detailed in the bottom drawing on page 184. We did this on the table saw fitted with a dado blade and set the rip fence as a stop.

Taper the stiles

The next step is to taper the stiles, as shown in the bottom photo. The taper starts 5" up from the bottom end and goes to the top of the stile, as shown in the drawing on page 184. See pages 84–87 for more on tapering on the jointer.

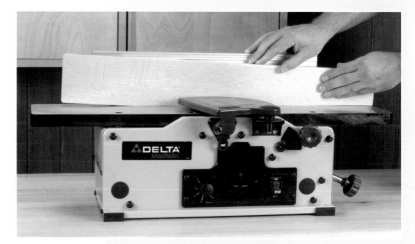

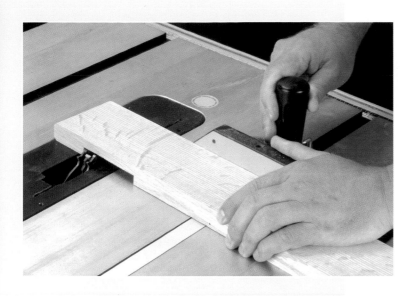

Cut the angled half-laps

The most accurate way to cut the angled half-laps in the top rail is to use the actual stiles to lay out the position and angle of the joints. To do this, temporarily assemble the stiles to the bottom rail and then place this assembly on the back of the top rail. Use a pencil to transfer the angled stiles onto the top rail. Then adjust your miter gauge to match this angle and make a pass; repeat for the opposite angled notch, resetting your miter gauge as needed. Once you've cut the angled edge of the half-lap, return your miter gauge to 90 degrees and finish cutting the half-lap, taking care to sneak up on a tight fit.

EXPLODED VIEW

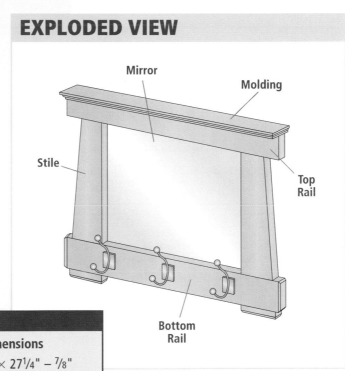

Mirror

Molding

Stile

Top Rail

Bottom Rail

MATERIALS LIST

Part	Quantity	Dimensions
Stiles	2	$4" \times 27\frac{1}{4}" - \frac{7}{8}"$
Top rail	1	$3\frac{1}{4}" \times 34" - \frac{7}{8}"$
Bottom rail	1	$4" \times 34" - \frac{7}{8}"$
Molding	1	$1\frac{3}{4}" \times 36" - \frac{7}{8}"$
Mirror	1	$\frac{1}{4}"$ thick, cut to fit
Hooks	3	Brass

Assemble the frame

With all the half-laps cut, you can assemble the frame. Apply glue to both sides of each half-lap and assemble the frame. Apply clamps at each joint; use scraps of wood (as shown in the top photo) to help distribute the clamping pressure. Allow the frame to dry overnight before removing the clamps.

Rout the rabbet for the mirror

The next step is to rout the rabbet in the back of the frame to accept the mirror, as shown in the middle photo. Use a router fitted with a $3/8$" rabbeting bit, and set it slightly deeper than the thickness of the mirror you're using. Rout along the inside perimeter of the frame, and then square up the corners with a chisel.

HALL MIRROR DETAILS

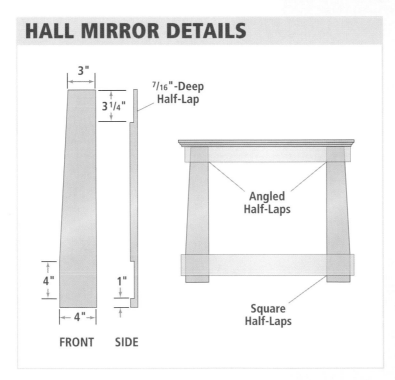

3"

$7/16$"-Deep Half-Lap

$3\frac{1}{4}$"

4"

1"

4"

FRONT   SIDE

Angled Half-Laps

Square Half-Laps

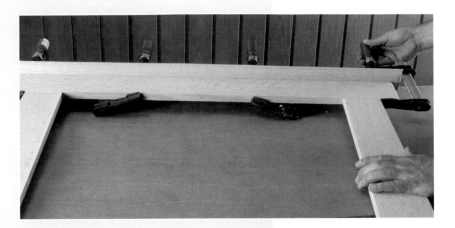

Add the top molding

Now you can make and attach the top molding. It's just a strip of wood with the front edge and ends profiled with a $3/8$" roundover bit, set to leave a $1/16$" shoulder. Secure the molding to the top of the frame with glue and clamps, as shown in the top photo.

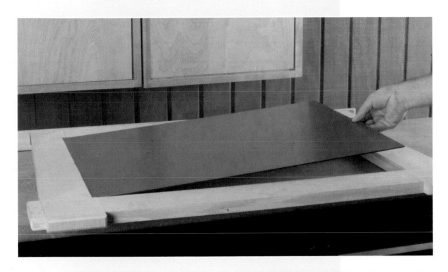

Install the mirror

At this point it's best to finish-sand the frame and apply the finish of your choice. If you'll be installing a mirror, take the finished frame to a glass shop and have them cut a mirror to fit the frame. When you get the mirror and frame back from the glass shop, apply a small bead of silicone caulk around the inside corner of the rabbet (silicone caulk has excellent adhesive properties). Then set the mirror in place as shown in the middle photo.

Add the hooks

Finally, if you're adding hooks, install them now. Take care to drill pilot holes for the screws, as these are often made of brass and will break easily. A little paraffin or paste wax on the threads will help the screws drive in more easily and also help reduce the chance of breakage.

Plant Stand

Although we originally designed this stand for plants, it can be used to store or display almost anything. A simple design with a cleaver adjustable shelf system combines to create an easy-to-build, attractive, and practical project. The plant stand consists of 4 posts that are tapered on the bottom, 10 shelf supports ($^1/_2$" dowels), and 3 shelves, as illustrated in the Exploded View drawing on the opposite page. The undersides of the shelves are notched to fit over the dowel supports. This allows you to easily reconfigure the stand while still providing solid shelving.

Lay out the dowel holes

To build the plant stand, start by cutting the parts to size per the materials list on the opposite page. Then lay out the locations of the dowel holes on the posts as described in the detail drawing at the bottom of page 188. Note that you should end up with two bookmatched pairs of posts. Centerpunch each dowel location, as shown in the middle photo, to prevent the drill bit from wandering.

Drill the dowel holes

Now you can drill the dowel holes in each post. You can do this on the drill press (as shown here) and set the depth stop to $^3/_4$" and drill the holes. Alternatively, you can do this with a portable drill—just make sure to use some sort of depth stop.

Taper the leg bottoms

With all the dowel holes drilled, the next step is to taper the bottoms of the posts, as shown in the top photo. The taper starts 5" up from the bottom of each leg and tapers down to half the thickness of the post. Note that the tapers are on one face only and need to be laid out and cut to create book-matched pairs. For more on tapering a post, see pages 84–87.

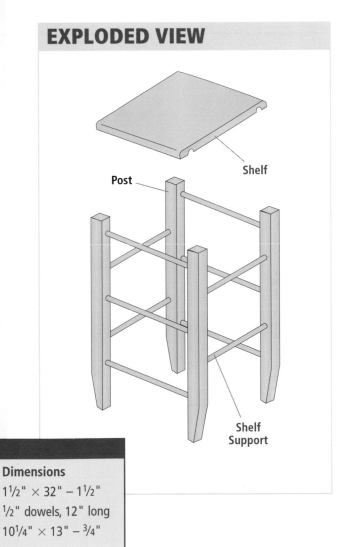

EXPLODED VIEW

Shelf

Post

Shelf
Support

MATERIALS LIST

Part	Quantity	Dimensions
Posts	4	$1\frac{1}{2}" \times 32" - 1\frac{1}{2}"$
Shelf supports	10	$\frac{1}{2}"$ dowels, 12" long
Shelves	3	$10\frac{1}{4}" \times 13" - \frac{3}{4}"$

Chamfer the tops of the posts

Before you assemble the stand, chamfer the tops of the posts. We used a laminate trimmer fitted with a chamfering bit, set to create a $1/4$"-wide chamfer, as shown in the top photo.

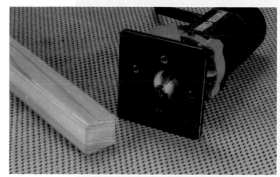

Assemble the stand

Now the stand can be assembled. Start by applying glue inside the dowel holes on a pair of bookmatched posts. Insert the dowels and rotate each dowel to spread the glue. Apply clamps and allow the side to dry overnight. Repeat for the opposite side of the stand. When both halves of the stand are dry, connect the two halves by spreading glue inside the dowel holes and inserting the dowels. Apply clamps (as shown in the middle photo), and allow to dry overnight.

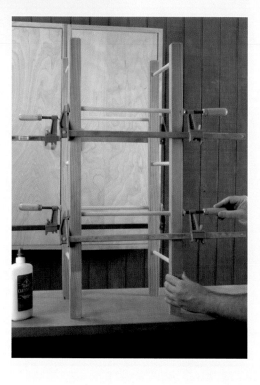

PLANT STAND DETAILS

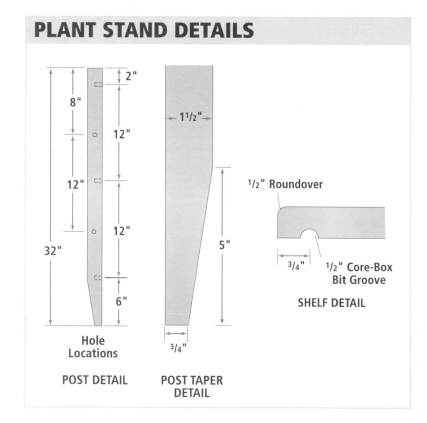

2"
8"
12"
12"
12"
12"
32"
6"

Hole Locations

POST DETAIL

$1^1/2$"

5"

$3/4$"

POST TAPER DETAIL

$1/2$" Roundover

$3/4$" $1/2$" Core-Box Bit Groove

SHELF DETAIL

Glue up the shelves

While the glue is drying on the stand, go ahead and glue up sufficient stock to create the three shelves as shown in the top photo. Allow the glue to dry overnight before cutting the shelves to finished width and length.

Rout the shelf grooves and roundovers

The shelves are designed to fit over the support dowels. The half-moon-shaped grooves in the underside of the shelves are cut with a $1/2$" core-box bit, fitted in a router in a router table, as shown in the middle photo. The groove is centered $1/2$" in from two opposite ends, as illustrated in the drawing on the opposite page. Rout two grooves in each shelf, and then round over the top edges with a $3/8$" roundover bit, as shown in the middle inset photo.

Add the shelves

All that's left is to add the shelves to the stand. You can simply let them rest in place on top of the shelf supports, or you can attach them permanently by driving screws up through the dowel supports and into the underside of the shelves, as shown in the bottom photo. Just make sure that you first drill pilots holes for the screws.

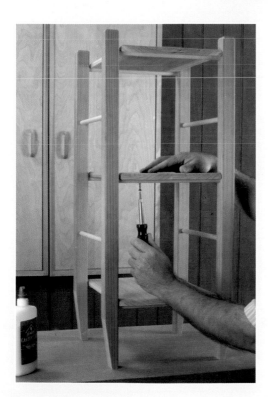

INDEX

METRIC EQUIVALENCY CHART

Inches to millimeters and centimeters

inches	mm	cm	inches	cm	inches	cm
1/8	3	0.3	9	22.9	30	76.2
1/4	6	0.6	10	25.4	31	78.7
3/8	10	1.0	11	27.9	32	81.3
1/2	13	1.3	12	30.5	33	83.8
5/8	16	1.6	13	33.0	34	86.4
3/4	19	1.9	14	35.6	35	88.9
7/8	22	2.2	15	38.1	36	91.4
1	25	2.5	16	40.6	37	94.0
1 1/4	32	3.2	17	43.2	38	96.5
1 1/2	38	3.8	18	45.7	39	99.1
1 3/4	44	4.4	19	48.3	40	101.6
2	51	5.1	20	50.8	41	104.1
2 1/2	64	6.4	21	53.3	42	106.7
3	76	7.6	22	55.9	43	109.2
3 1/2	89	8.9	23	58.4	44	111.8
4	102	10.2	24	61.0	45	114.3
4 1/2	114	11.4	25	63.5	46	116.8
5	127	12.7	26	66.0	47	119.4
6	152	15.2	27	68.6	48	121.9
7	178	17.8	28	71.1	49	124.5
8	203	20.3	29	73.7	50	127.0

mm = millimeters   cm = centimeters

Jointer and Planer Fundamentals Photography Credits

Photos courtesy of Delta Machinery (www.deltamachinery.com): page 9 (middle), page 18 (top), page 39 (top), page 47 (top).

Photos courtesy of General Manufacturing (www.general.ca): page 11, page 18 (middle), page 24, page 33.

Photos courtesy of Jet Tools (www.jettools.com): page 10, page 23, page 26 (middle and bottom), page 27 (bottom left), page 28 (top and middle right), page 29 (middle), page 32, page 34 (middle), page 42 (bottom left), page 43 (top and middle).

Photos courtesy of Laguna Tools (www.lagunatools.com): page 35 (all).

Photo courtesy of Makita U.S.A. (www.makita.com): page 68 (bottom).

Photos courtesy of Powermatic (www.powermatic.com): page 3, page 5, page 16 (all), page 18 (bottom), page 27 (bottom right), page 28 (middle and bottom left, bottom right), page 29 (bottom), page 30 (bottom), page 34 (top).

Photos courtesy of Ryobi Tools (www.ryobitools.com): page 1, page 22.

Photos courtesy of Sunhill Machinery (www.sunhillmachinery.com): page 41 (all), page 44 (bottom).

Photo courtesy of Triton Manufacturing (www.triton.com.au): page 47 (middle).